nickelodeon

降去神通

AVATAR

THE LAST AIRBENDER

Created by
Bryan Konietzko
Michael Dante DiMartino

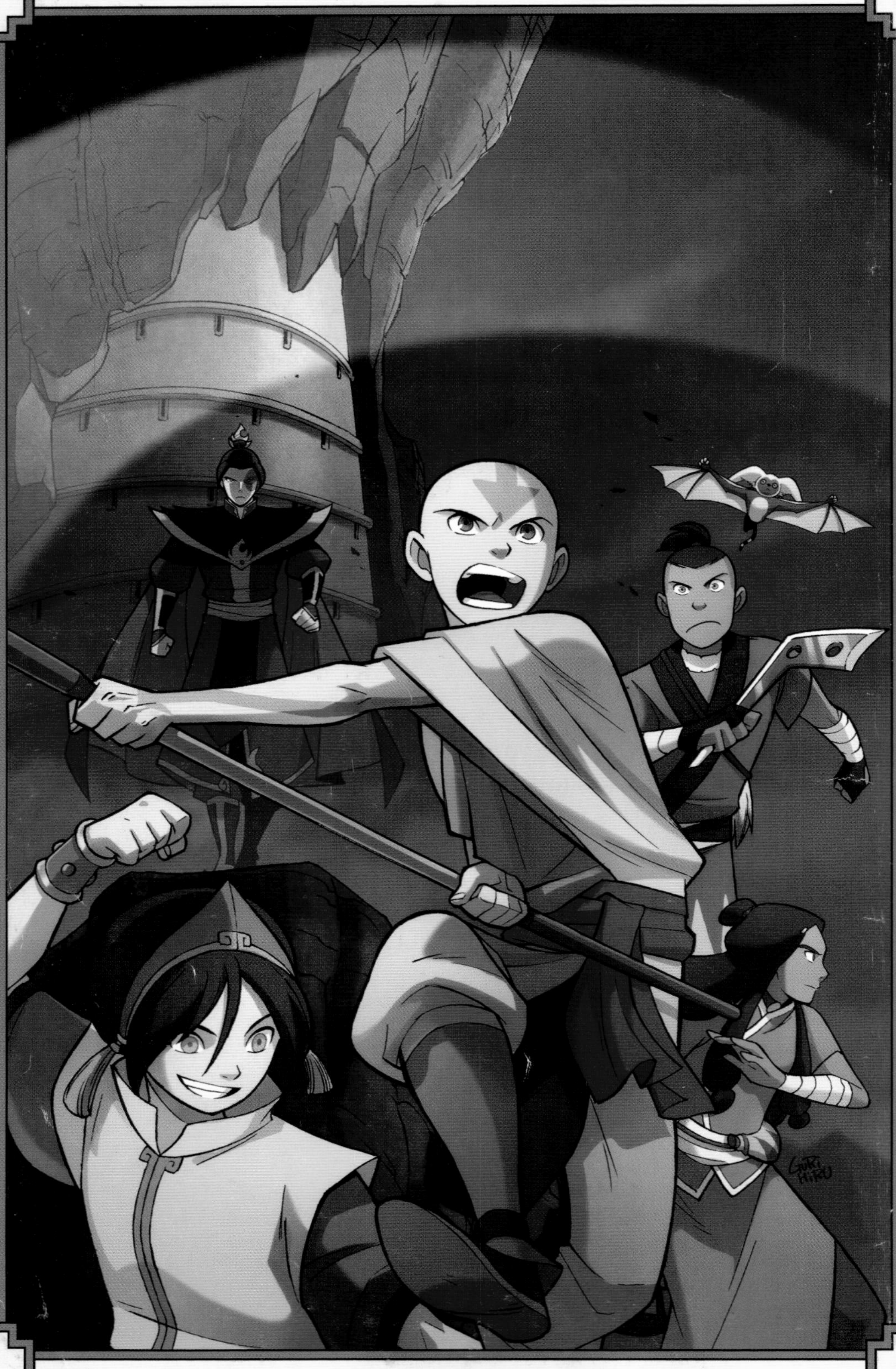
GURI HIRU

nickelodeon

降去神通

AVATAR

THE LAST AIRBENDER

THE PROMISE · PART TWO

script
GENE LUEN YANG

art and cover
GURIHIRU

lettering
MICHAEL HEISLER

DARK HORSE BOOKS

publisher
MIKE RICHARDSON

designer
JUSTIN COUCH

assistant editor
BRENDAN WRIGHT

editor
DAVE MARSHALL

Special thanks to Linda Lee, Kat van Dam, James Salerno,
and Joan Hilty at Nickelodeon, to Samantha Robertson,
and to Bryan Konietzko and Michael Dante DiMartino.

Published by
Dark Horse Books
A division of
Dark Horse Comics, Inc.
10956 SE Main Street
Milwaukie, OR 97222

DarkHorse.com
Nick.com

To find a comics shop in your area, call the Comic Shop
Locator Service toll-free at (888) 266-4226.

First edition: May 2012
ISBN 978-1-59582-875-0

1 3 5 7 9 10 8 6 4 2
Printed at Midas Printing International, Ltd., Huizhou, China

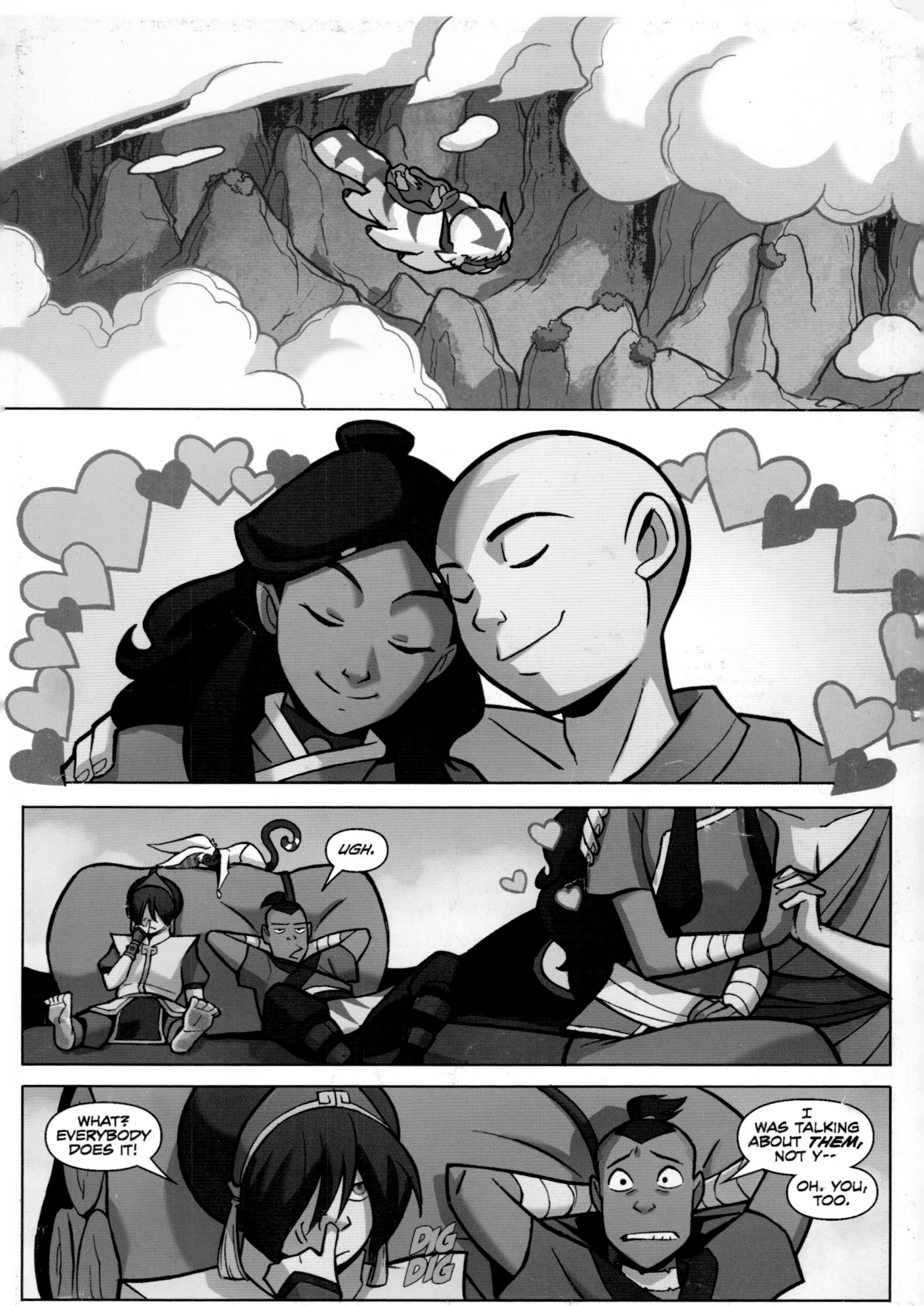
UGH.
WHAT? EVERYBODY DOES IT!
I WAS TALKING ABOUT *THEM,* NOT Y--
OH. YOU, TOO.
DIG DIG

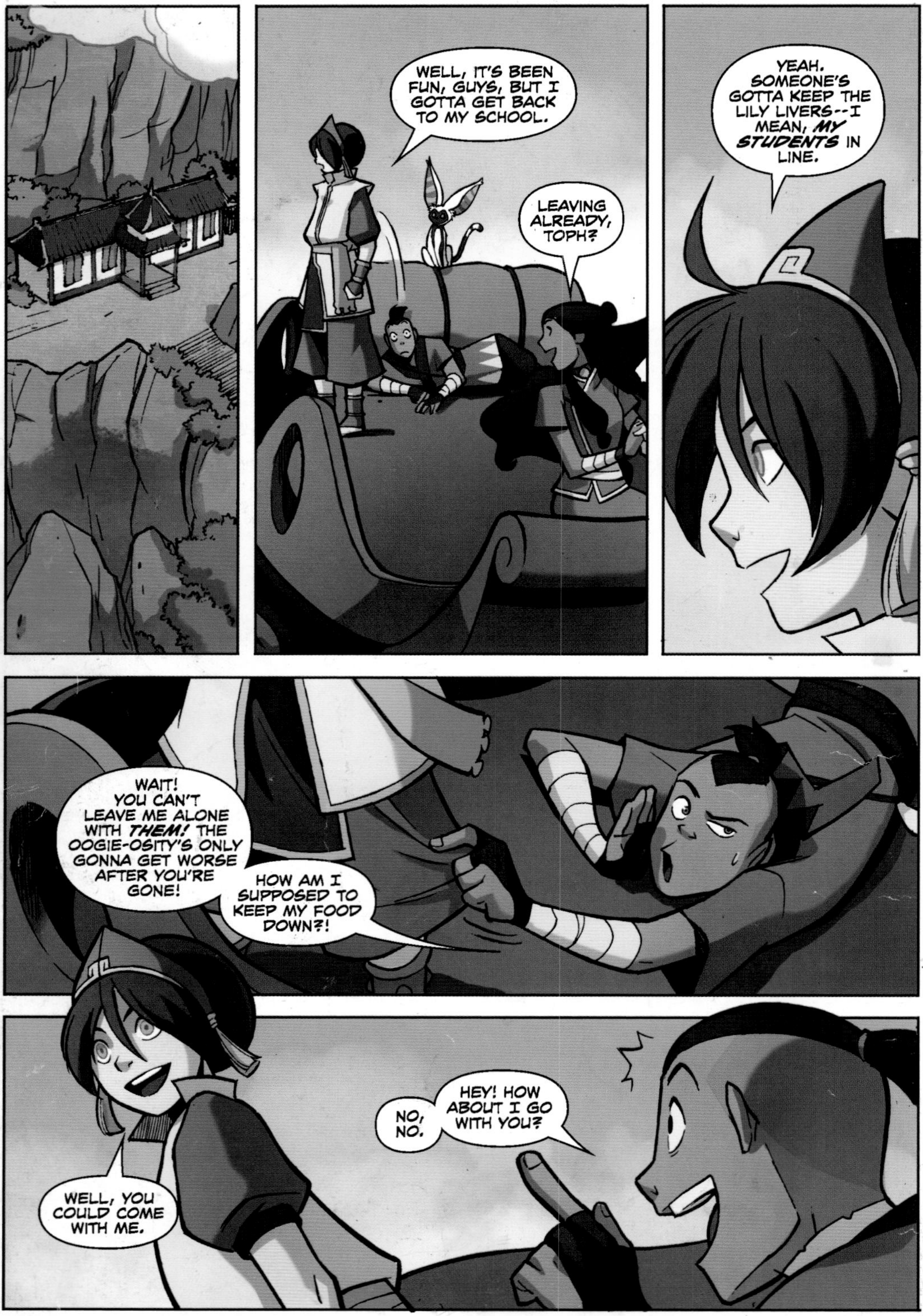

WELL, IT'S BEEN FUN, GUYS, BUT I GOTTA GET BACK TO MY SCHOOL.
LEAVING ALREADY, TOPH?
YEAH. SOMEONE'S GOTTA KEEP THE LILY LIVERS--I MEAN, *MY STUDENTS* IN LINE.
WAIT! YOU CAN'T LEAVE ME ALONE WITH *THEM!* THE OOGIE-OSITY'S ONLY GONNA GET WORSE AFTER YOU'RE GONE!
HOW AM I SUPPOSED TO KEEP MY FOOD DOWN?!
WELL, YOU COULD COME WITH ME.
HEY! HOW ABOUT I GO WITH YOU?
NO, NO.

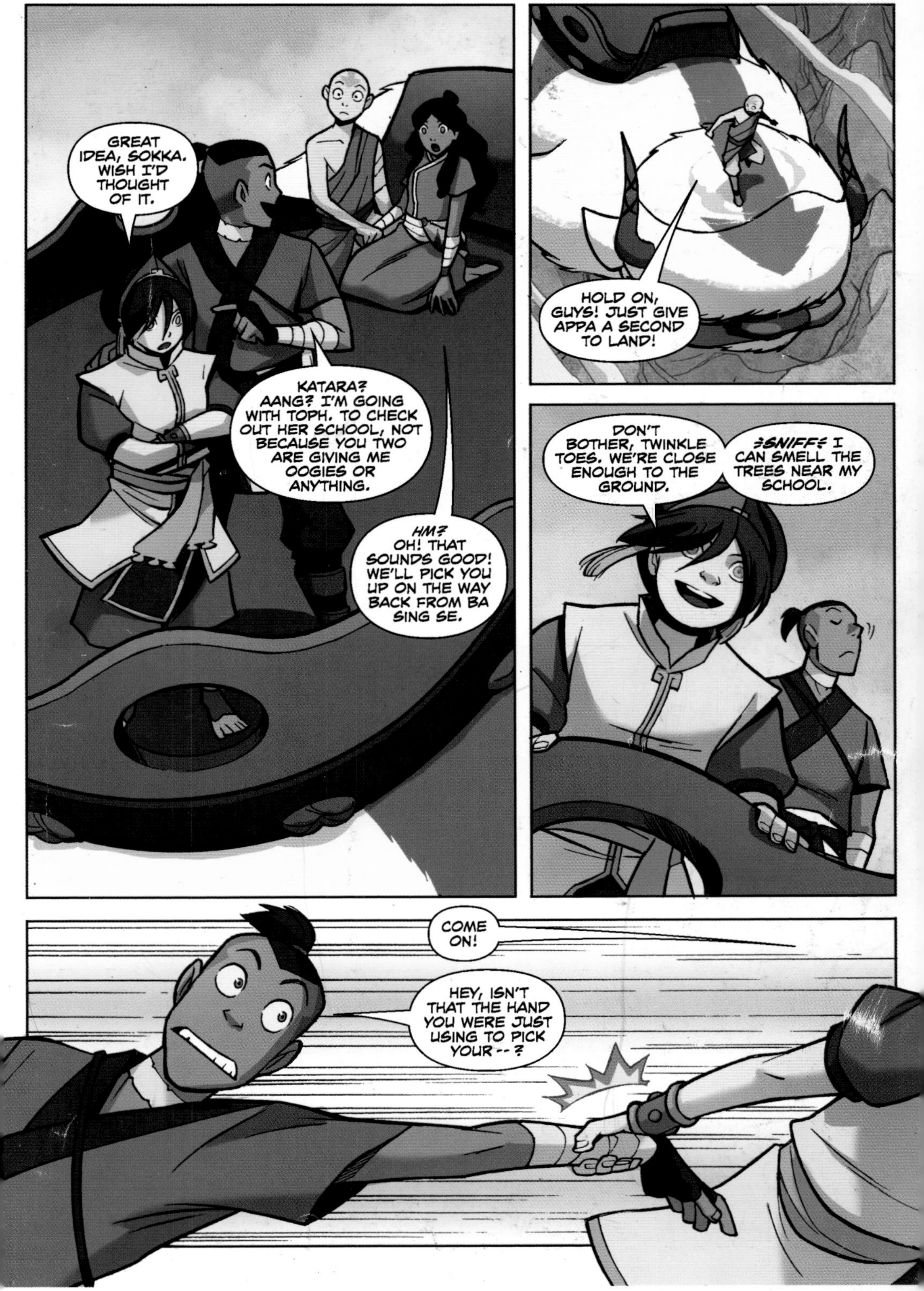
GREAT IDEA, SOKKA. WISH I'D THOUGHT OF IT.
KATARA? AANG? I'M GOING WITH TOPH. TO CHECK OUT HER SCHOOL, NOT BECAUSE YOU TWO ARE GIVING ME OOGIES OR ANYTHING.
HM? OH! THAT SOUNDS GOOD! WE'LL PICK YOU UP ON THE WAY BACK FROM BA SING SE.
HOLD ON, GUYS! JUST GIVE APPA A SECOND TO LAND!
DON'T BOTHER, TWINKLE TOES. WE'RE CLOSE ENOUGH TO THE GROUND.
SNIFF I CAN SMELL THE TREES NEAR MY SCHOOL.
COME ON!
HEY, ISN'T THAT THE HAND YOU WERE JUST USING TO PICK YOUR--?

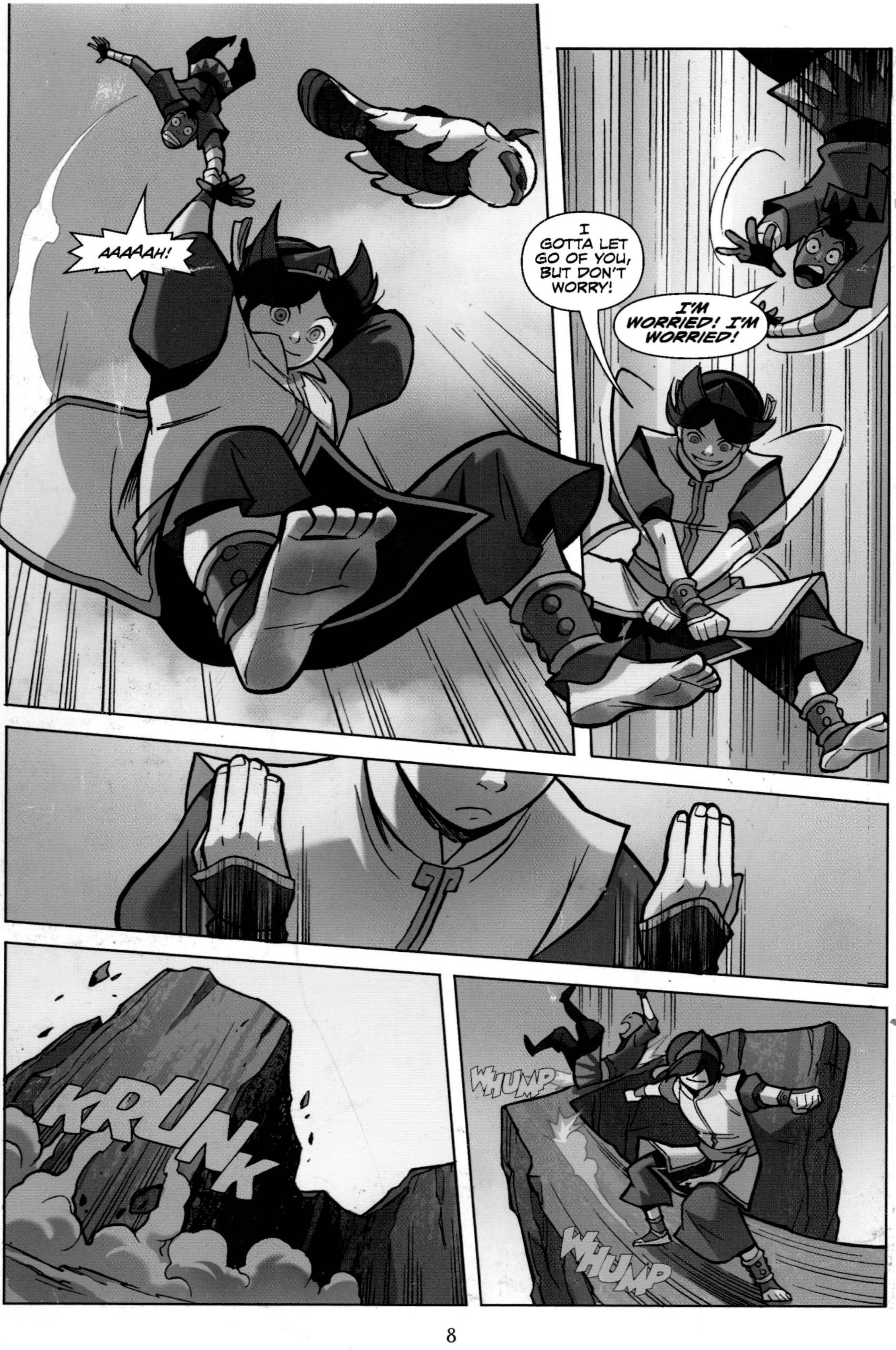

AAAAAH!
I GOTTA LET GO OF YOU, BUT DON'T WORRY!
I'M WORRIED! I'M WORRIED!
KRUNK
WHUMP
WHUMP

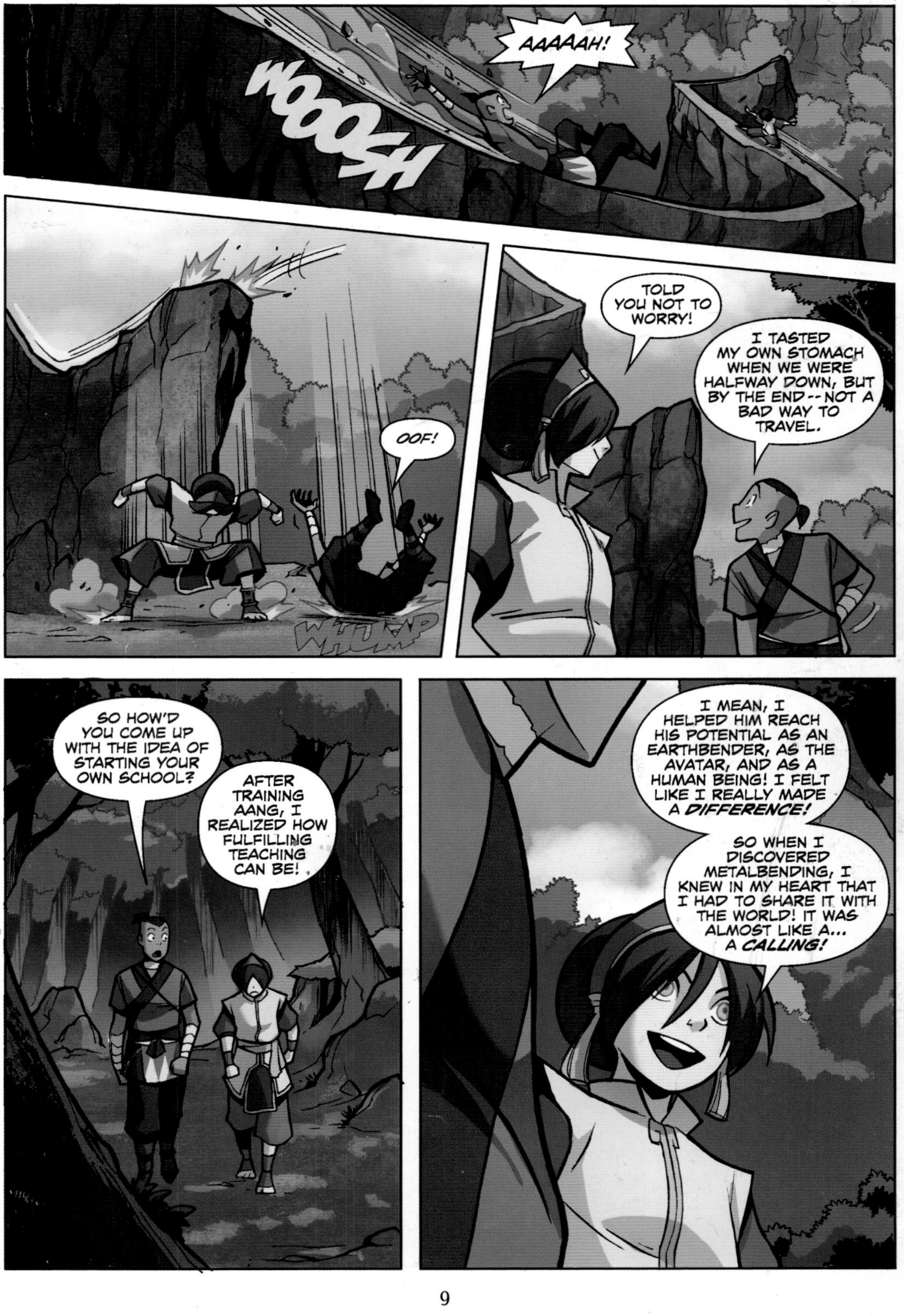
AAAAAH!
WOOOSH
OOF!
WHUMP
TOLD YOU NOT TO WORRY!
I TASTED MY OWN STOMACH WHEN WE WERE HALFWAY DOWN, BUT BY THE END--NOT A BAD WAY TO TRAVEL.
SO HOW'D YOU COME UP WITH THE IDEA OF STARTING YOUR OWN SCHOOL?
AFTER TRAINING AANG, I REALIZED HOW FULFILLING TEACHING CAN BE!
I MEAN, I HELPED HIM REACH HIS POTENTIAL AS AN EARTHBENDER, AS THE AVATAR, AND AS A HUMAN BEING! I FELT LIKE I REALLY MADE A *DIFFERENCE!*
SO WHEN I DISCOVERED METALBENDING, I KNEW IN MY HEART THAT I HAD TO SHARE IT WITH THE WORLD! IT WAS ALMOST LIKE A... A *CALLING!*

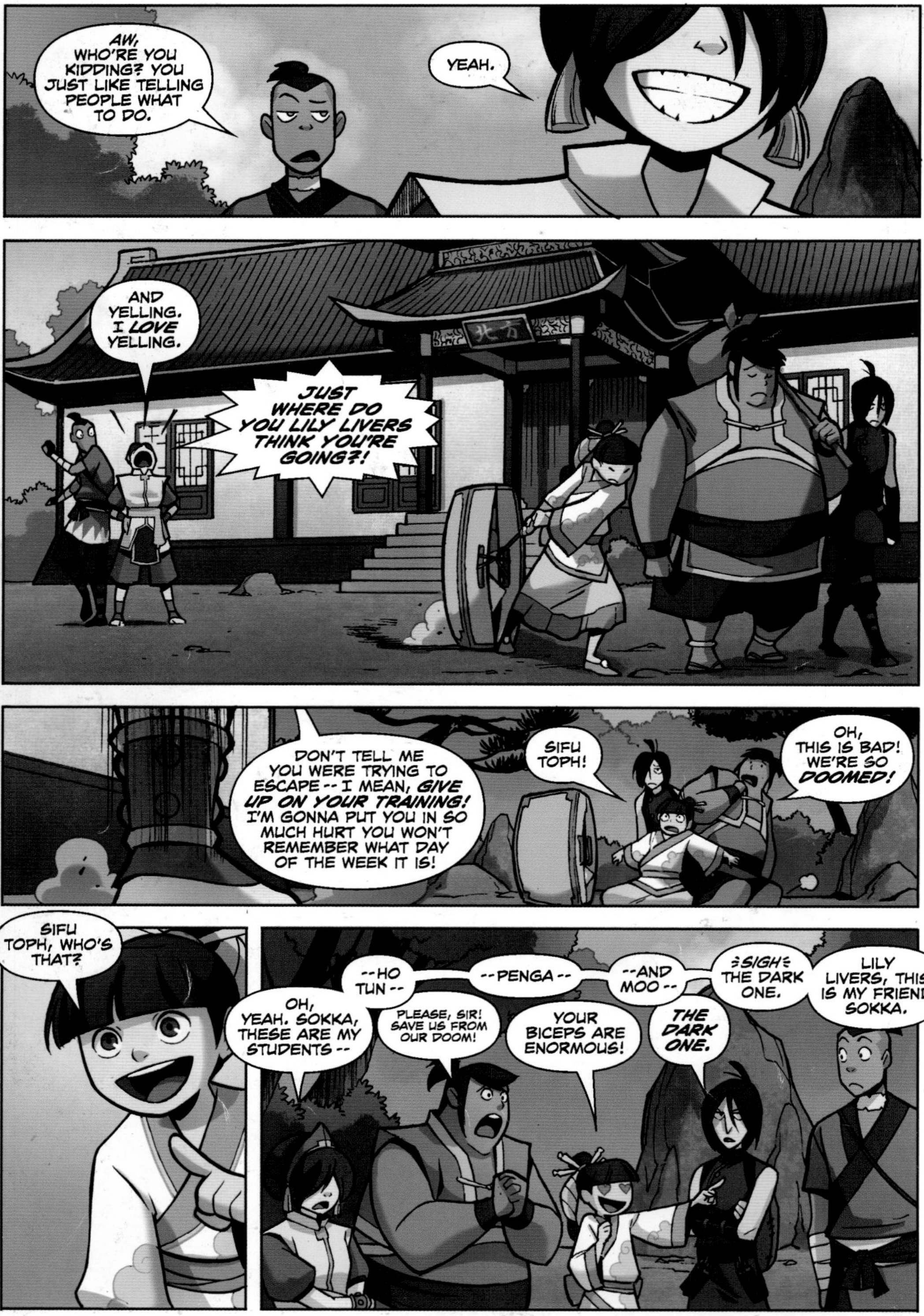
AW, WHO'RE YOU KIDDING? YOU JUST LIKE TELLING PEOPLE WHAT TO DO.
YEAH.
AND YELLING. I *LOVE* YELLING.
JUST WHERE DO YOU LILY LIVERS THINK YOU'RE GOING?!
DON'T TELL ME YOU WERE TRYING TO ESCAPE -- I MEAN, *GIVE UP ON YOUR TRAINING!* I'M GONNA PUT YOU IN SO MUCH HURT YOU WON'T REMEMBER WHAT DAY OF THE WEEK IT IS!
SIFU TOPH!
OH, THIS IS BAD! WE'RE SO *DOOMED!*
SIFU TOPH, WHO'S THAT?
LILY LIVERS, THIS IS MY FRIEND SOKKA.
SIGH THE DARK ONE.
THE DARK ONE.
--AND MOO --
YOUR BICEPS ARE ENORMOUS!
-- PENGA --
PLEASE, SIR! SAVE US FROM OUR DOOM!
--HO TUN --
OH, YEAH. SOKKA, THESE ARE MY STUDENTS --

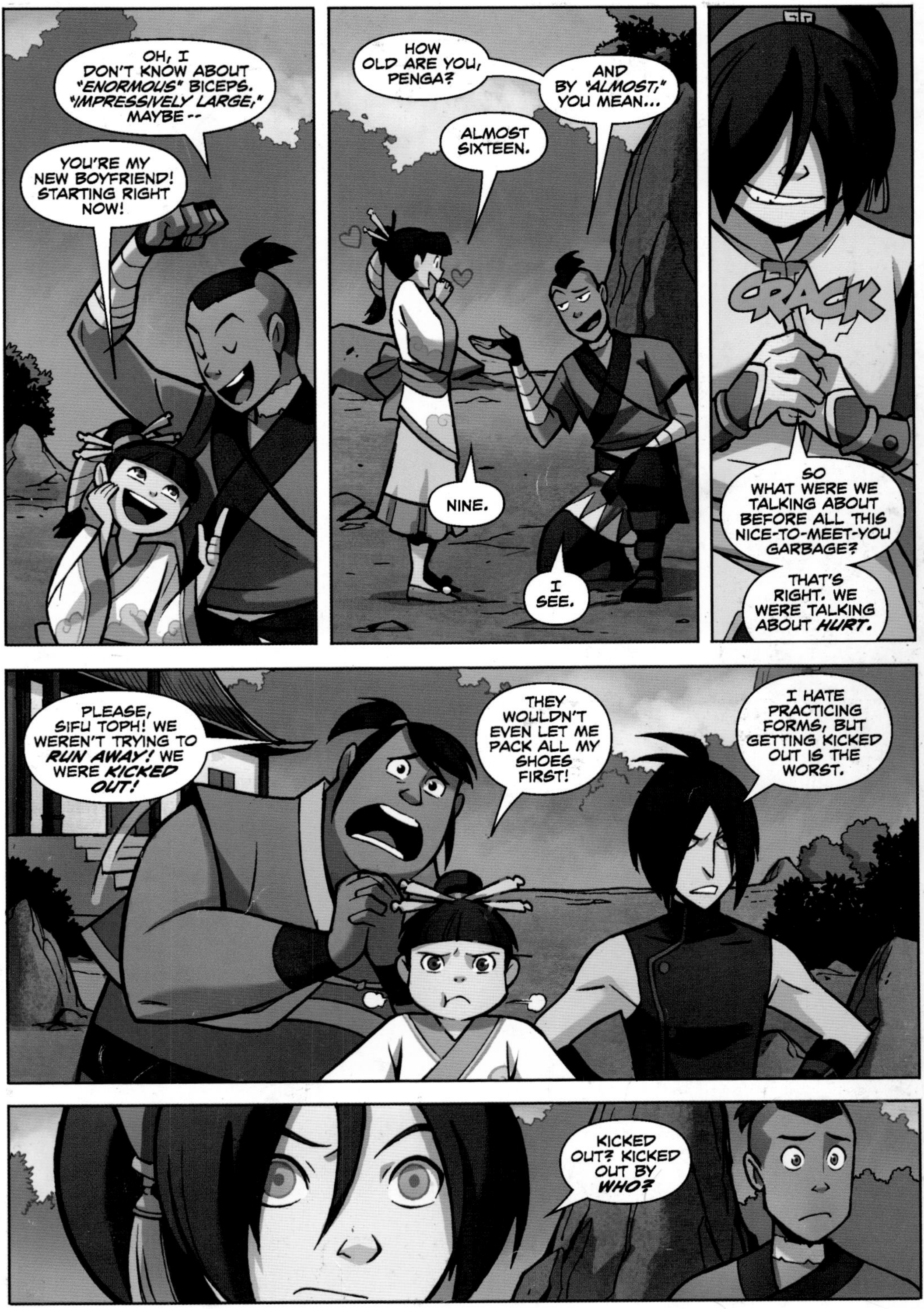

OH, I DON'T KNOW ABOUT "ENORMOUS" BICEPS. "IMPRESSIVELY LARGE," MAYBE --
YOU'RE MY NEW BOYFRIEND! STARTING RIGHT NOW!
HOW OLD ARE YOU, PENGA?
ALMOST SIXTEEN.
AND BY "ALMOST," YOU MEAN...
NINE.
I SEE.
CRACK
SO WHAT WERE WE TALKING ABOUT BEFORE ALL THIS NICE-TO-MEET-YOU GARBAGE?
THAT'S RIGHT. WE WERE TALKING ABOUT HURT.
PLEASE, SIFU TOPH! WE WEREN'T TRYING TO RUN AWAY! WE WERE KICKED OUT!
THEY WOULDN'T EVEN LET ME PACK ALL MY SHOES FIRST!
I HATE PRACTICING FORMS, BUT GETTING KICKED OUT IS THE WORST.
KICKED OUT? KICKED OUT BY WHO?

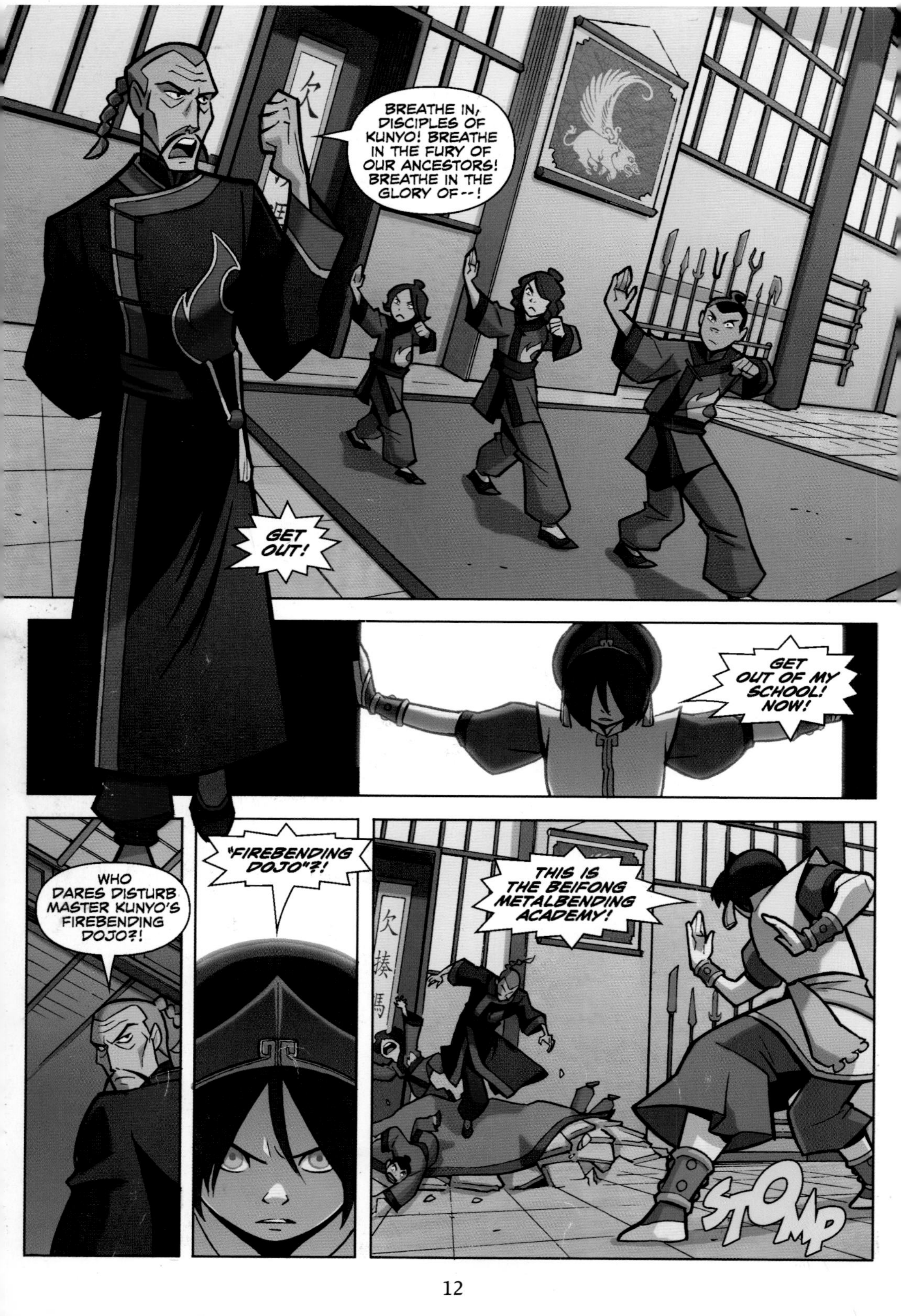
BREATHE IN, DISCIPLES OF KUNYO! BREATHE IN THE FURY OF OUR ANCESTORS! BREATHE IN THE GLORY OF--!
GET OUT!
GET OUT OF MY SCHOOL! NOW!
WHO DARES DISTURB MASTER KUNYO'S FIREBENDING DOJO?!
"FIREBENDING DOJO"?!
THIS IS THE BEIFONG METALBENDING ACADEMY!
STOMP

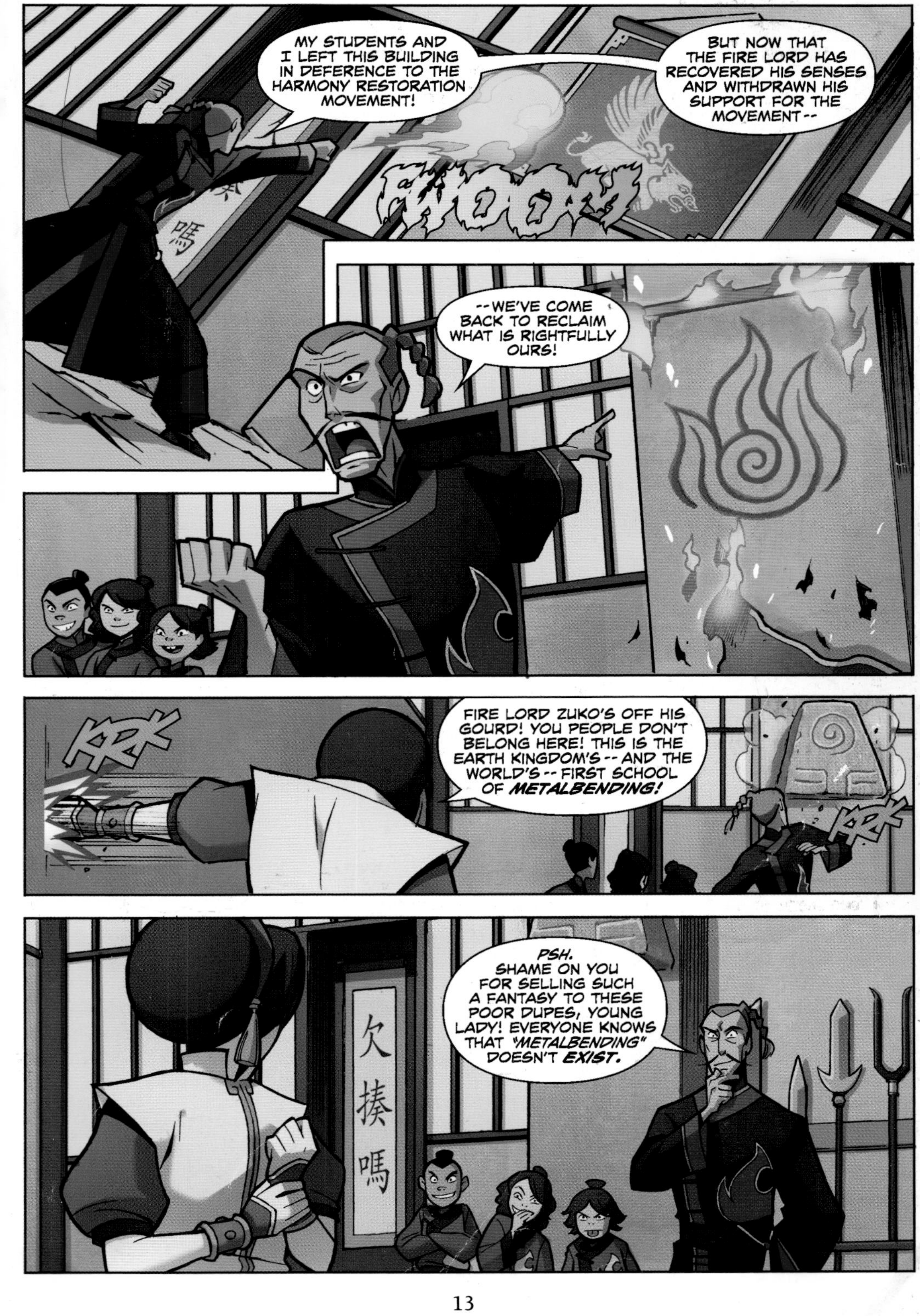
MY STUDENTS AND I LEFT THIS BUILDING IN DEFERENCE TO THE HARMONY RESTORATION MOVEMENT!
BUT NOW THAT THE FIRE LORD HAS RECOVERED HIS SENSES AND WITHDRAWN HIS SUPPORT FOR THE MOVEMENT--
FWOOM
--WE'VE COME BACK TO RECLAIM WHAT IS RIGHTFULLY OURS!
KRK
FIRE LORD ZUKO'S OFF HIS GOURD! YOU PEOPLE DON'T BELONG HERE! THIS IS THE EARTH KINGDOM'S--AND THE WORLD'S--FIRST SCHOOL OF *METALBENDING!*
KRK
PSH. SHAME ON YOU FOR SELLING SUCH A FANTASY TO THESE POOR DUPES, YOUNG LADY! EVERYONE KNOWS THAT *"METALBENDING"* DOESN'T *EXIST.*
欠揍嗎

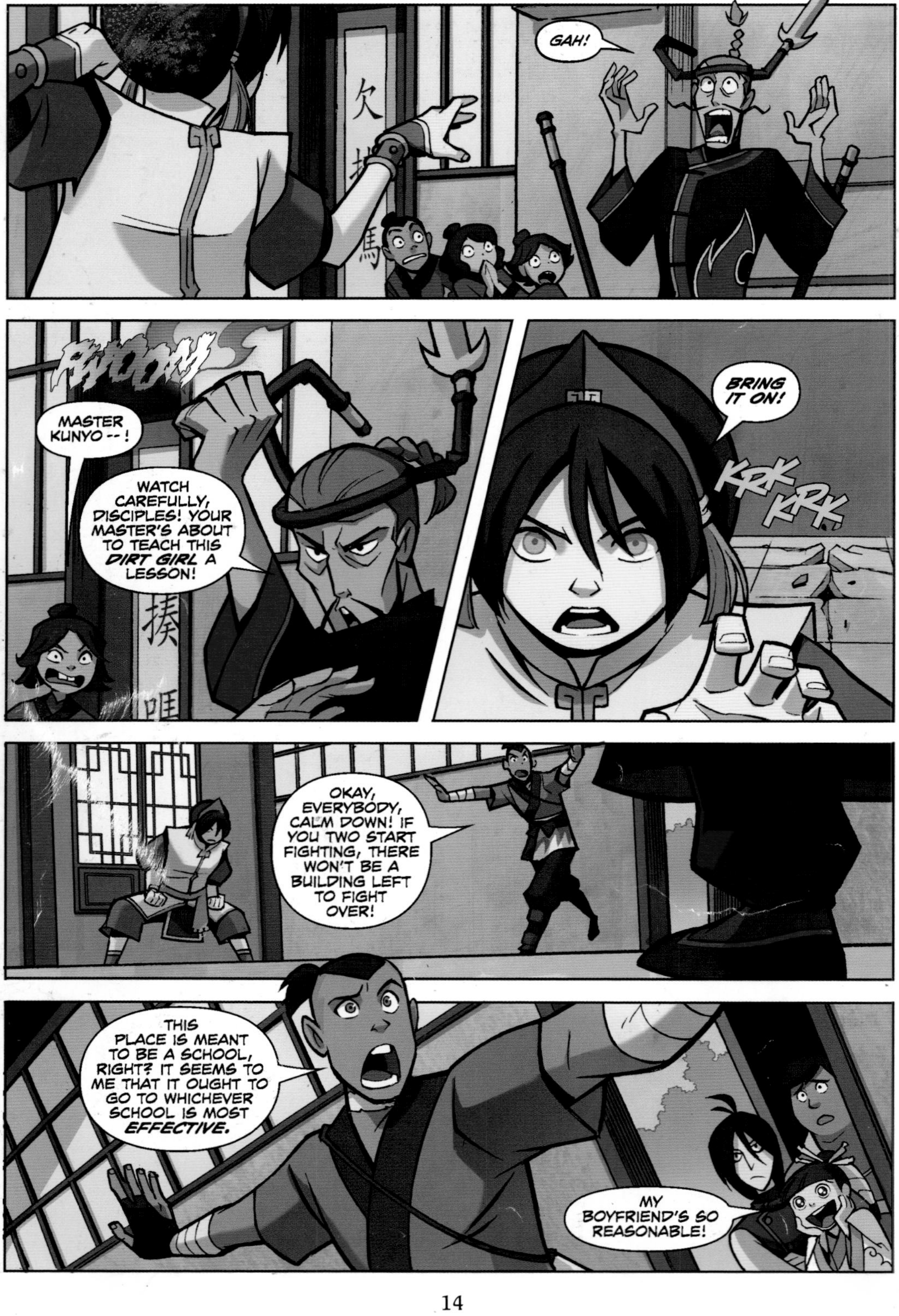
GAH!
FWOOM
MASTER KUNYO --!
WATCH CAREFULLY, DISCIPLES! YOUR MASTER'S ABOUT TO TEACH THIS *DIRT GIRL* A LESSON!
BRING IT ON!
KRK KRK
OKAY, EVERYBODY, CALM DOWN! IF YOU TWO START FIGHTING, THERE WON'T BE A BUILDING LEFT TO FIGHT OVER!
THIS PLACE IS MEANT TO BE A SCHOOL, RIGHT? IT SEEMS TO ME THAT IT OUGHT TO GO TO WHICHEVER SCHOOL IS MOST *EFFECTIVE.*
MY BOYFRIEND'S SO REASONABLE!

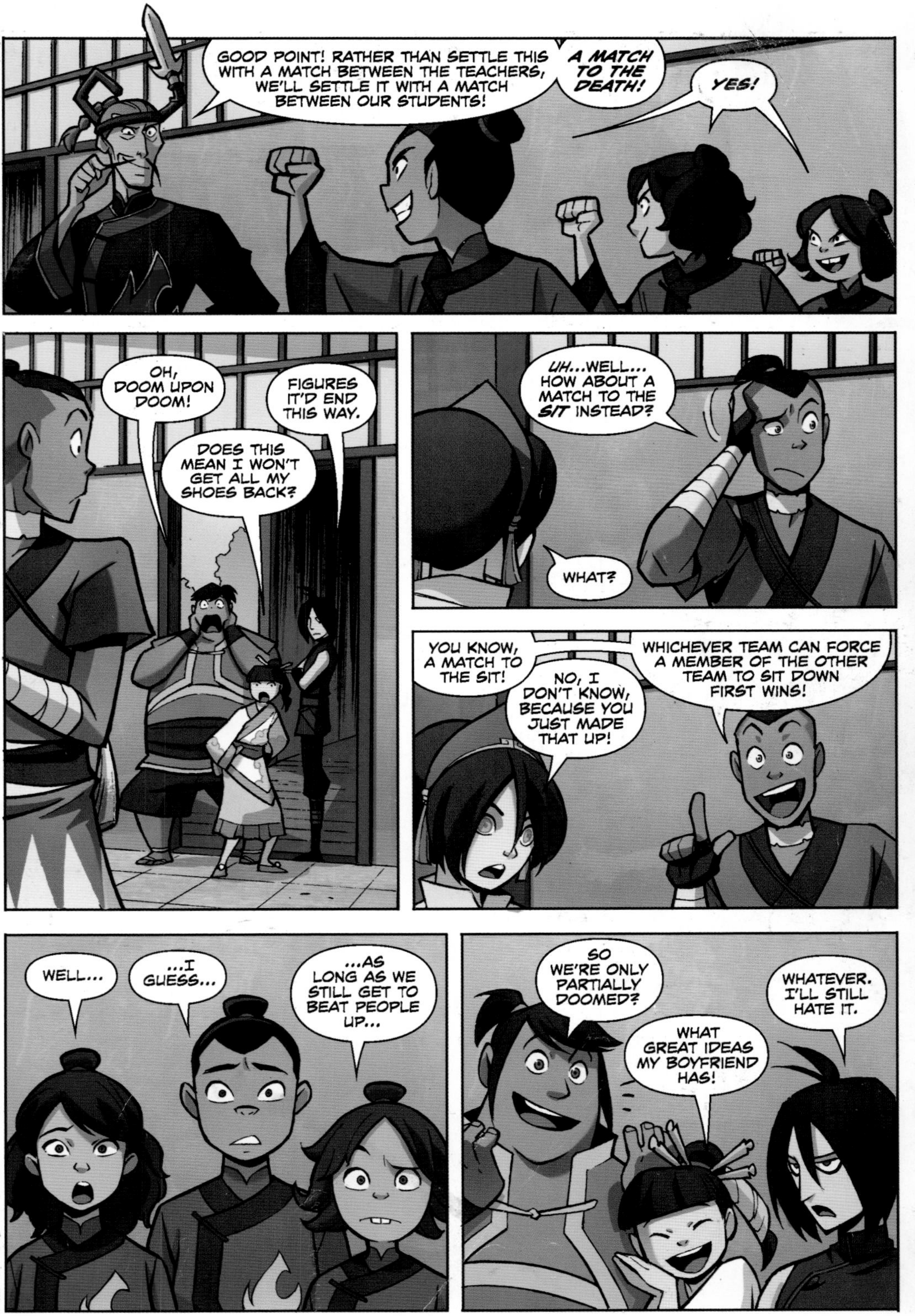
GOOD POINT! RATHER THAN SETTLE THIS WITH A MATCH BETWEEN THE TEACHERS, WE'LL SETTLE IT WITH A MATCH BETWEEN OUR STUDENTS!
A MATCH TO THE DEATH!
YES!
OH, DOOM UPON DOOM!
FIGURES IT'D END THIS WAY.
DOES THIS MEAN I WON'T GET ALL MY SHOES BACK?
UH...WELL... HOW ABOUT A MATCH TO THE SIT INSTEAD?
WHAT?
YOU KNOW, A MATCH TO THE SIT!
NO, I DON'T KNOW, BECAUSE YOU JUST MADE THAT UP!
WHICHEVER TEAM CAN FORCE A MEMBER OF THE OTHER TEAM TO SIT DOWN FIRST WINS!
WELL...
...I GUESS...
...AS LONG AS WE STILL GET TO BEAT PEOPLE UP...
SO WE'RE ONLY PARTIALLY DOOMED?
WHAT GREAT IDEAS MY BOYFRIEND HAS!
WHATEVER. I'LL STILL HATE IT.

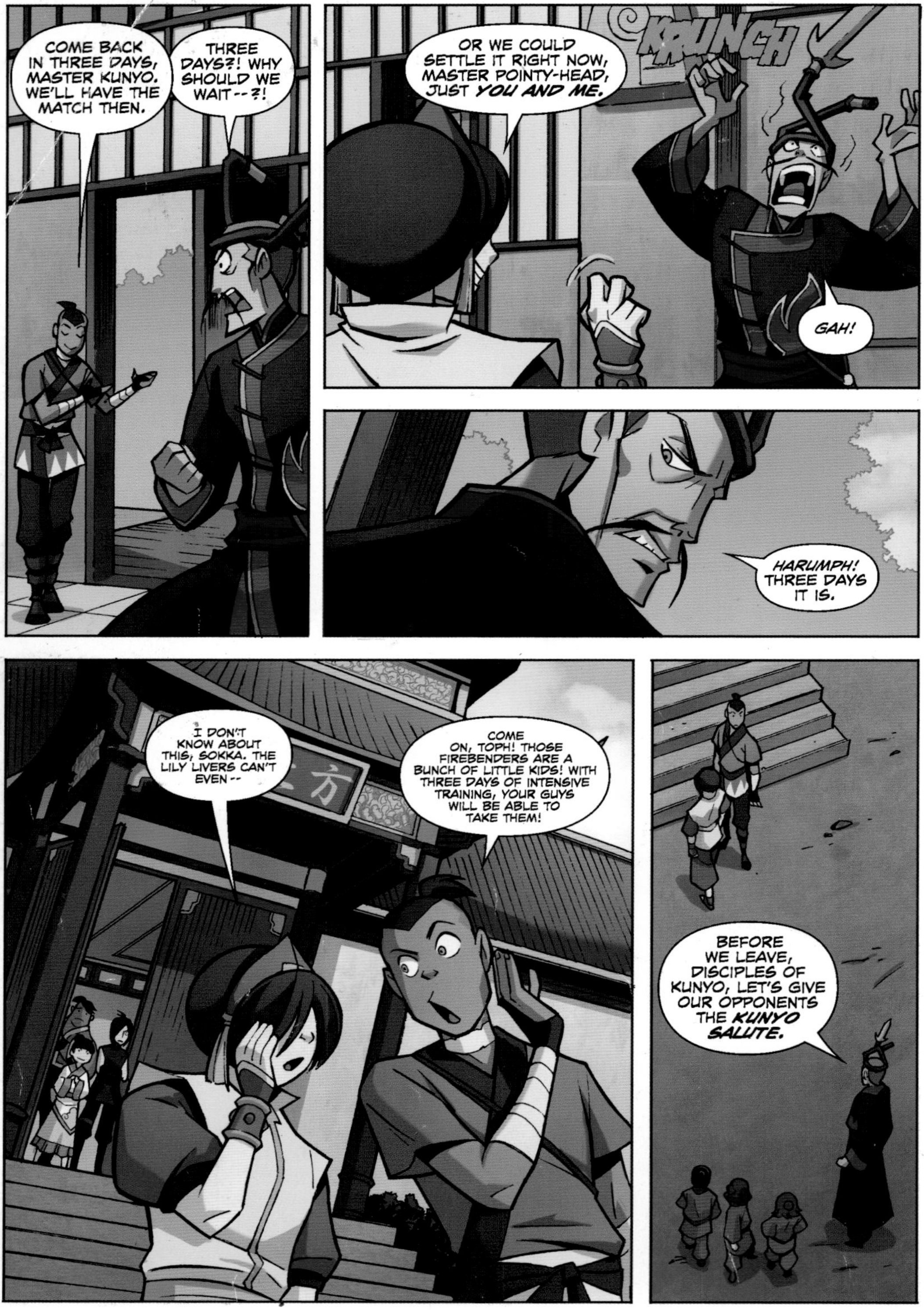
COME BACK IN THREE DAYS, MASTER KUNYO. WE'LL HAVE THE MATCH THEN.
THREE DAYS?! WHY SHOULD WE WAIT--?!
OR WE COULD SETTLE IT RIGHT NOW, MASTER POINTY-HEAD, JUST YOU AND ME.
KRUNCH
GAH!
HARUMPH! THREE DAYS IT IS.
I DON'T KNOW ABOUT THIS, SOKKA. THE LILY LIVERS CAN'T EVEN--
COME ON, TOPH! THOSE FIREBENDERS ARE A BUNCH OF LITTLE KIDS! WITH THREE DAYS OF INTENSIVE TRAINING, YOUR GUYS WILL BE ABLE TO TAKE THEM!
BEFORE WE LEAVE, DISCIPLES OF KUNYO, LET'S GIVE OUR OPPONENTS THE KUNYO SALUTE.

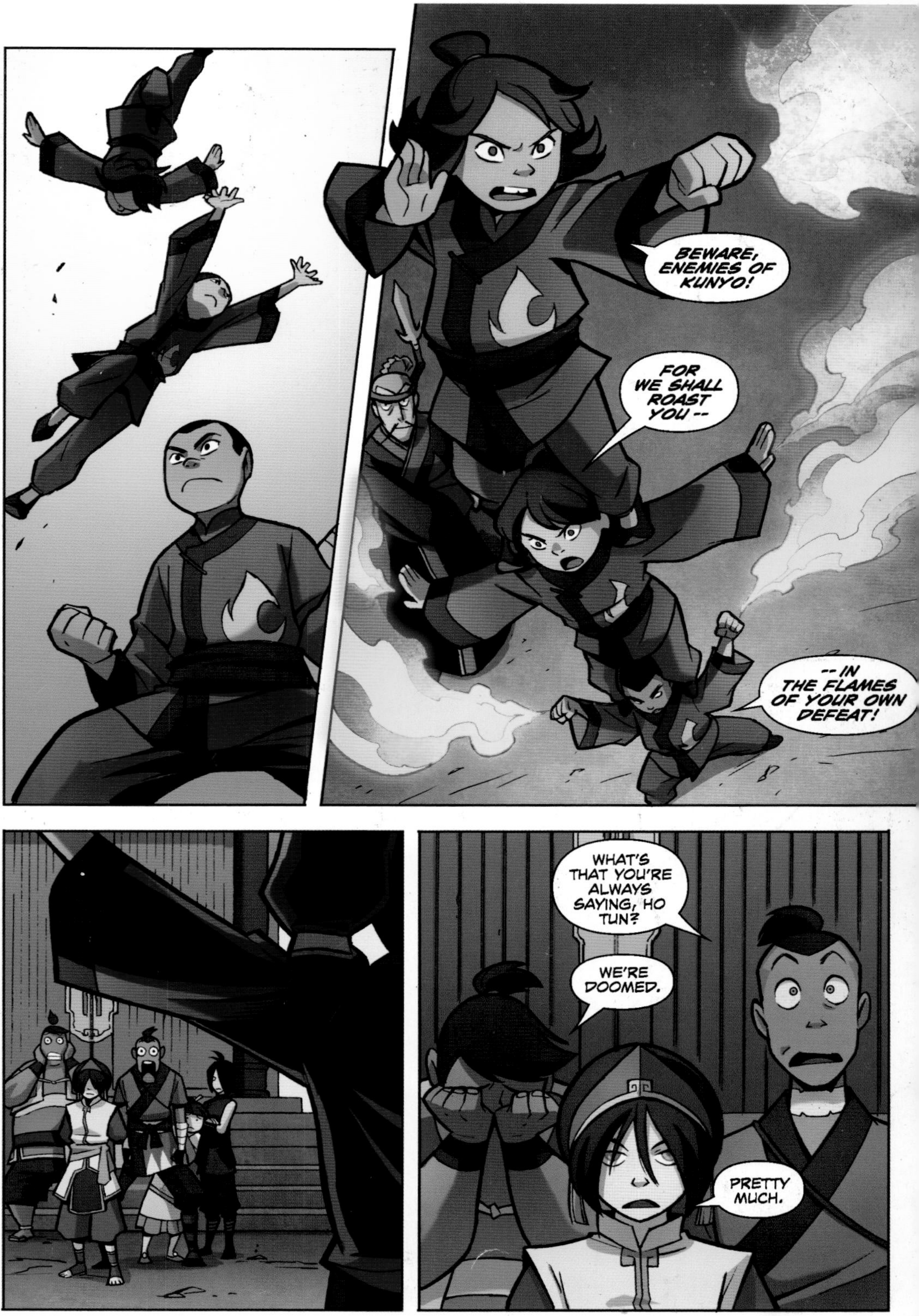
BEWARE, ENEMIES OF KUNYO!
FOR WE SHALL ROAST YOU --
-- IN THE FLAMES OF YOUR OWN DEFEAT!
WHAT'S THAT YOU'RE ALWAYS SAYING, HO TUN?
WE'RE DOOMED.
PRETTY MUCH.

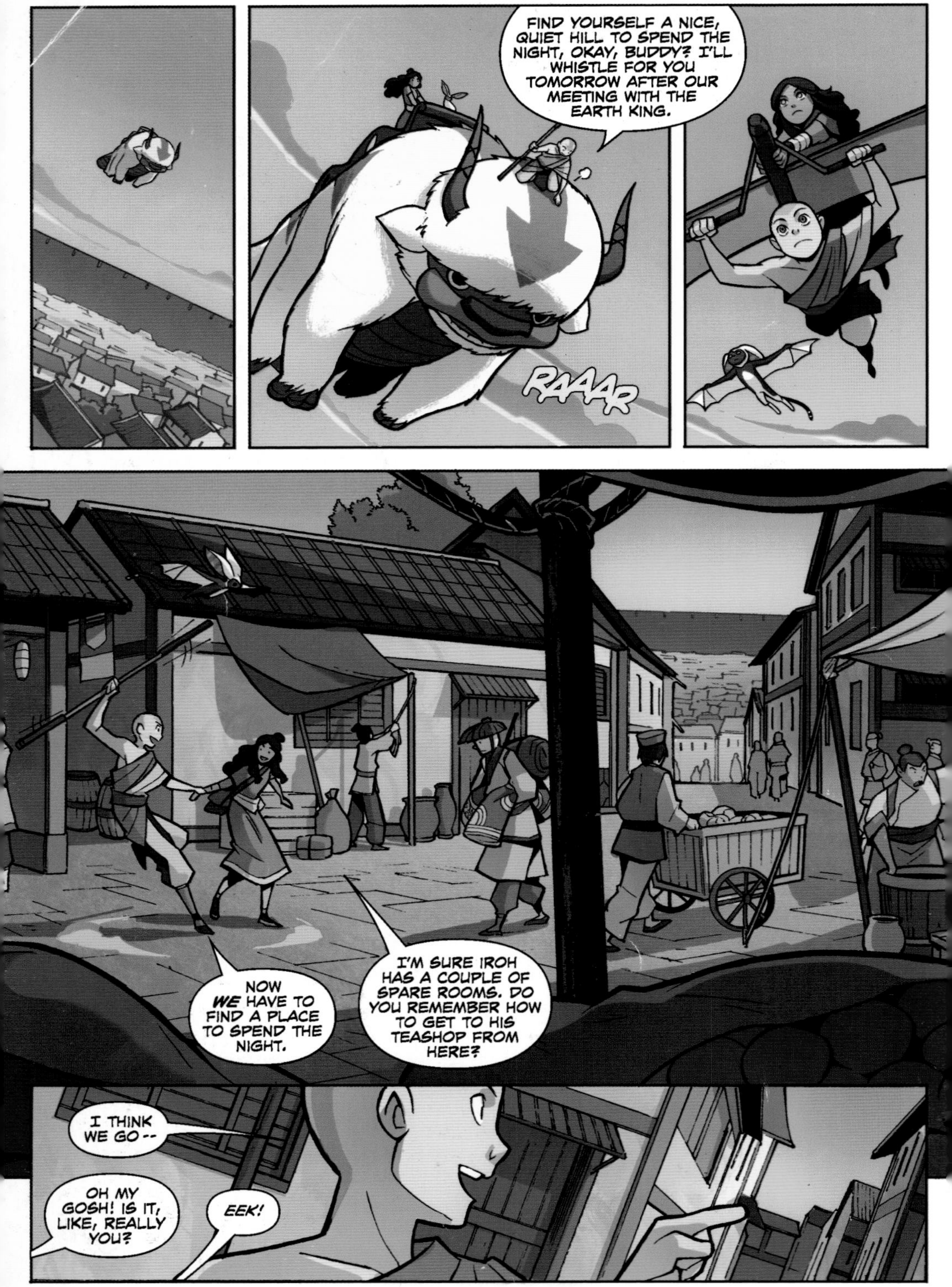
FIND YOURSELF A NICE, QUIET HILL TO SPEND THE NIGHT, OKAY, BUDDY? I'LL WHISTLE FOR YOU TOMORROW AFTER OUR MEETING WITH THE EARTH KING.
RAAAR
NOW *WE* HAVE TO FIND A PLACE TO SPEND THE NIGHT.
I'M SURE IROH HAS A COUPLE OF SPARE ROOMS. DO YOU REMEMBER HOW TO GET TO HIS TEASHOP FROM HERE?
I THINK WE GO --
OH MY GOSH! IS IT, LIKE, REALLY YOU?
EEK!

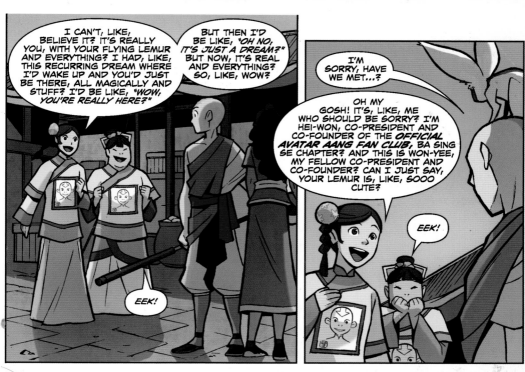

I CAN'T, LIKE, BELIEVE IT? IT'S REALLY YOU, WITH YOUR FLYING LEMUR AND EVERYTHING? I HAD, LIKE, THIS RECURRING DREAM WHERE I'D WAKE UP AND YOU'D JUST BE THERE, ALL MAGICALLY AND STUFF? I'D BE LIKE, "WOW, YOU'RE REALLY HERE?"

BUT THEN I'D BE LIKE, "OH NO, IT'S JUST A DREAM?" BUT NOW, IT'S REAL AND EVERYTHING? SO, LIKE, WOW?

EEK!

I'M SORRY, HAVE WE MET...?

OH MY GOSH! IT'S, LIKE, ME WHO SHOULD BE SORRY? I'M HEI-WON, CO-PRESIDENT AND CO-FOUNDER OF THE *OFFICIAL AVATAR AANG FAN CLUB*, BA SING SE CHAPTER? AND THIS IS WON-YEE, MY FELLOW CO-PRESIDENT AND CO-FOUNDER? CAN I JUST SAY, YOUR LEMUR IS, LIKE, SOOO CUTE?

EEK!

WOW! DID YOU HEAR THAT? THEY STARTED A FAN CLUB FOR ME!

WONDERFUL.

NICE TO MEET YOU BOTH! I'M AANG! MY LEMUR'S NAME IS MOMO.

"MOMO" IS, LIKE, THE CUTEST NAME EVER?

EEK!

≩AHEM≩

OH! AND THIS IS KATARA!

≩AHEM!≩

MY *GIRLFRIEND* KATARA!

19

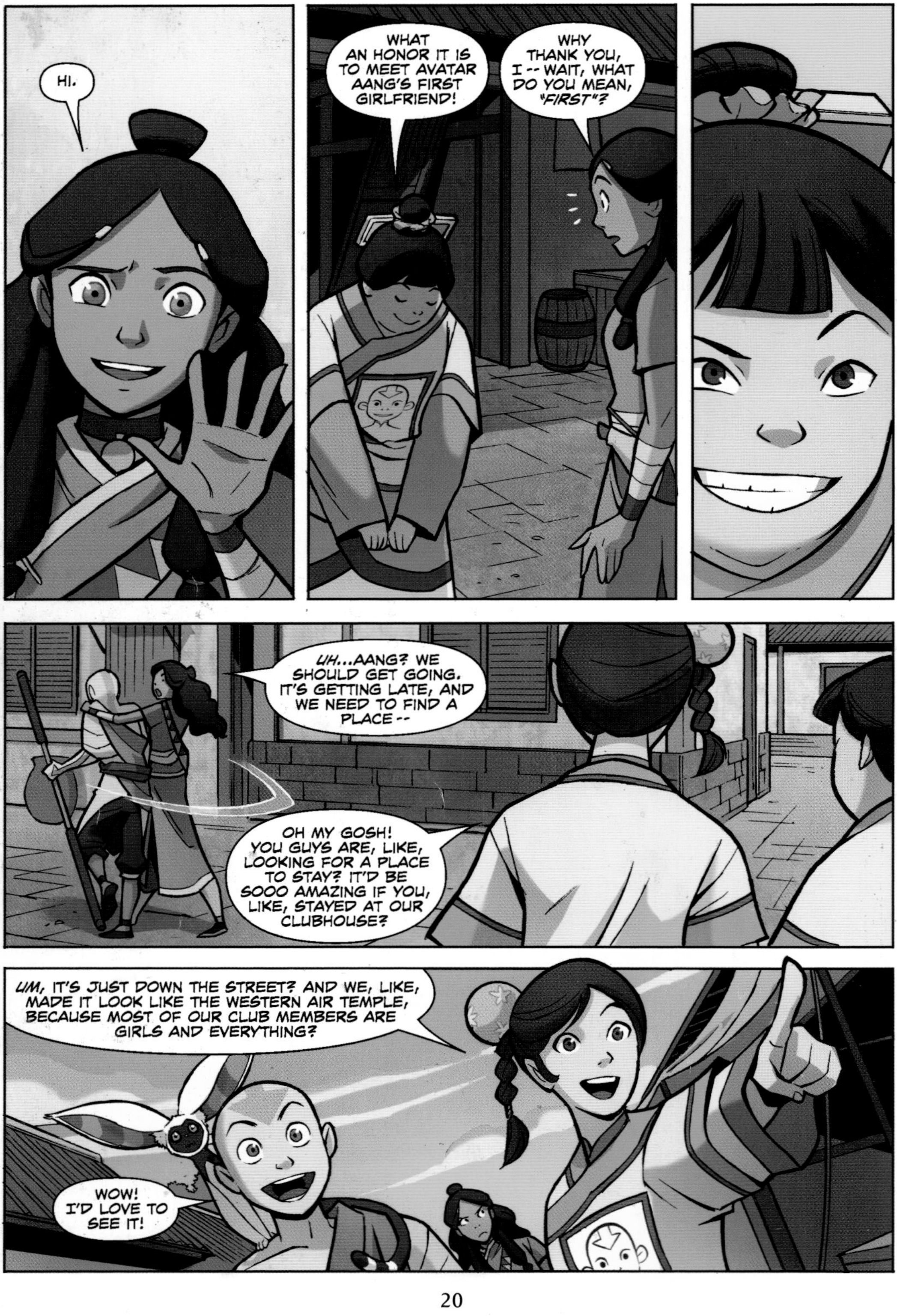
HI.
WHAT AN HONOR IT IS TO MEET AVATAR AANG'S FIRST GIRLFRIEND!
WHY THANK YOU, I -- WAIT, WHAT DO YOU MEAN, *"FIRST"*?
UH...AANG? WE SHOULD GET GOING. IT'S GETTING LATE, AND WE NEED TO FIND A PLACE --
OH MY GOSH! YOU GUYS ARE, LIKE, LOOKING FOR A PLACE TO STAY? IT'D BE SOOO AMAZING IF YOU, LIKE, STAYED AT OUR CLUBHOUSE?
UM, IT'S JUST DOWN THE STREET? AND WE, LIKE, MADE IT LOOK LIKE THE WESTERN AIR TEMPLE, BECAUSE MOST OF OUR CLUB MEMBERS ARE GIRLS AND EVERYTHING?
WOW! I'D LOVE TO SEE IT!

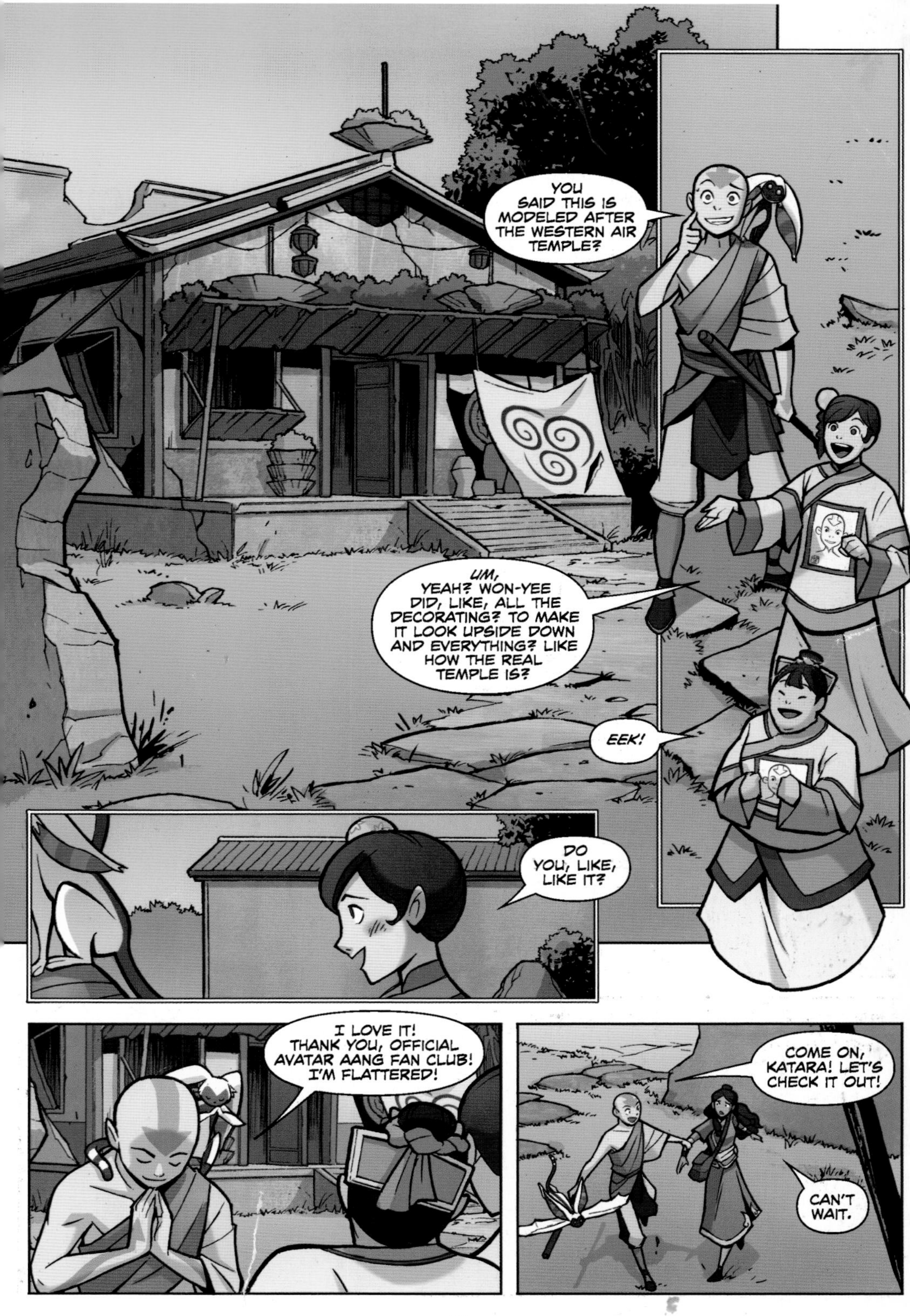
YOU SAID THIS IS MODELED AFTER THE WESTERN AIR TEMPLE?
UM, YEAH? WON-YEE DID, LIKE, ALL THE DECORATING? TO MAKE IT LOOK UPSIDE DOWN AND EVERYTHING? LIKE HOW THE REAL TEMPLE IS?
EEK!
DO YOU, LIKE, LIKE IT?
I LOVE IT! THANK YOU, OFFICIAL AVATAR AANG FAN CLUB! I'M FLATTERED!
COME ON, KATARA! LET'S CHECK IT OUT!
CAN'T WAIT.

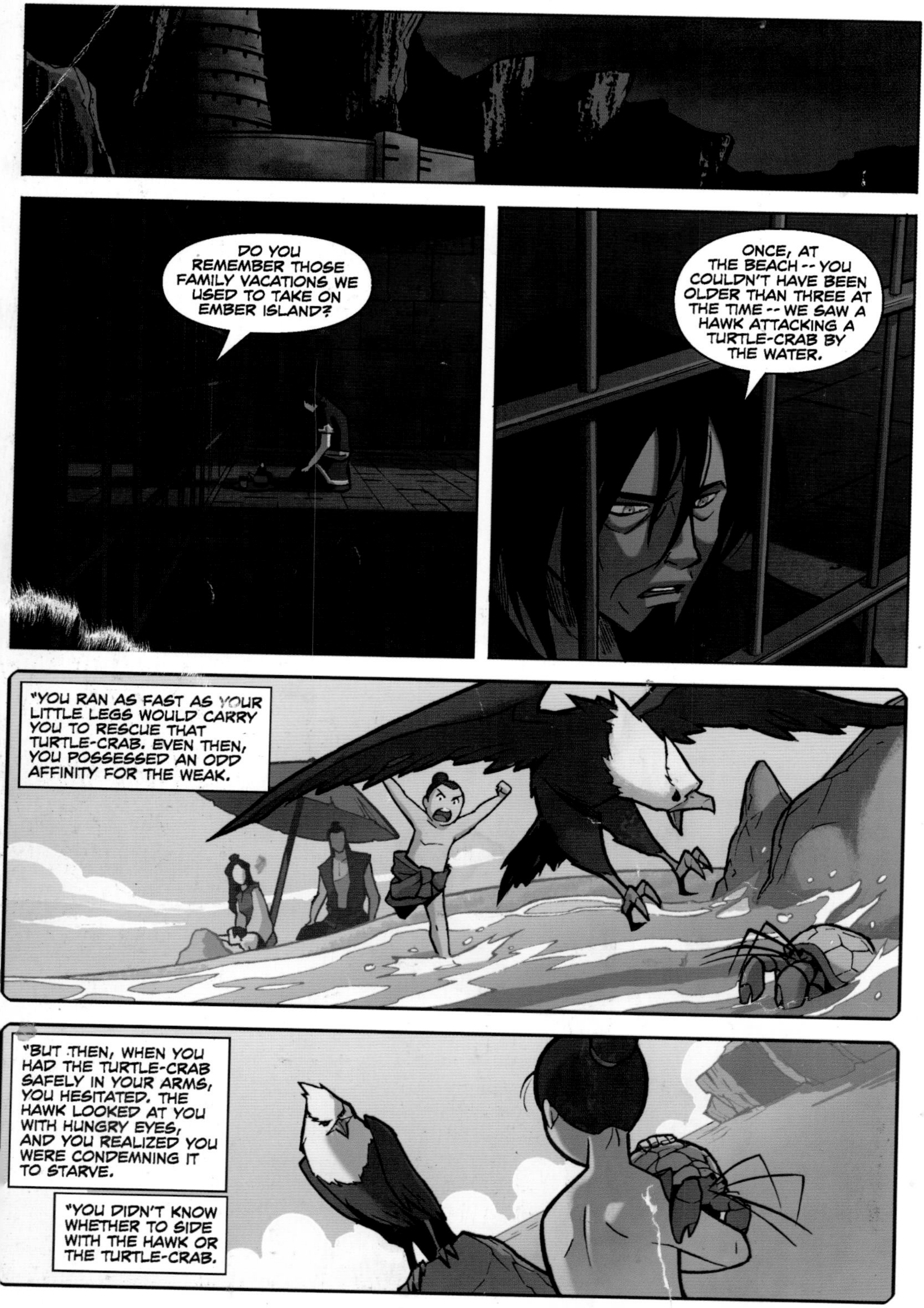
DO YOU REMEMBER THOSE FAMILY VACATIONS WE USED TO TAKE ON EMBER ISLAND?
ONCE, AT THE BEACH -- YOU COULDN'T HAVE BEEN OLDER THAN THREE AT THE TIME -- WE SAW A HAWK ATTACKING A TURTLE-CRAB BY THE WATER.
"YOU RAN AS FAST AS YOUR LITTLE LEGS WOULD CARRY YOU TO RESCUE THAT TURTLE-CRAB. EVEN THEN, YOU POSSESSED AN ODD AFFINITY FOR THE WEAK.
"BUT THEN, WHEN YOU HAD THE TURTLE-CRAB SAFELY IN YOUR ARMS, YOU HESITATED. THE HAWK LOOKED AT YOU WITH HUNGRY EYES, AND YOU REALIZED YOU WERE CONDEMNING IT TO STARVE.
"YOU DIDN'T KNOW WHETHER TO SIDE WITH THE HAWK OR THE TURTLE-CRAB.

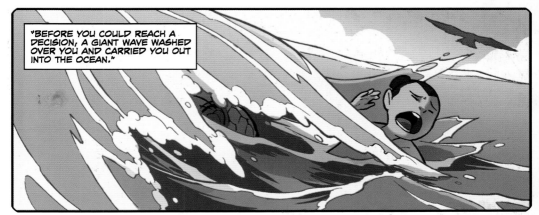

"BEFORE YOU COULD REACH A DECISION, A GIANT WAVE WASHED OVER YOU AND CARRIED YOU OUT INTO THE OCEAN."

I DOVE IN MYSELF TO SAVE YOU. YOU SPENT THE REST OF THE DAY IN YOUR MOTHER'S ARMS, VOMITING SEA-WATER.

SIP

I CAME HERE LOOKING FOR ADVICE. I WANT TO KNOW HOW YOU WERE ABLE TO SLEEP PEACEFULLY IN SPITE OF THE PRESSURES OF THE THRONE.

AND I TOLD YOU.

I DON'T SEE HOW AN OLD FAMILY MEMORY --

I'M TIRED, ZUKO. WE'RE DONE TALKING FOR NOW. PERHAPS WE WILL CONTINUE TOMORROW.

BRING MORE TEA.

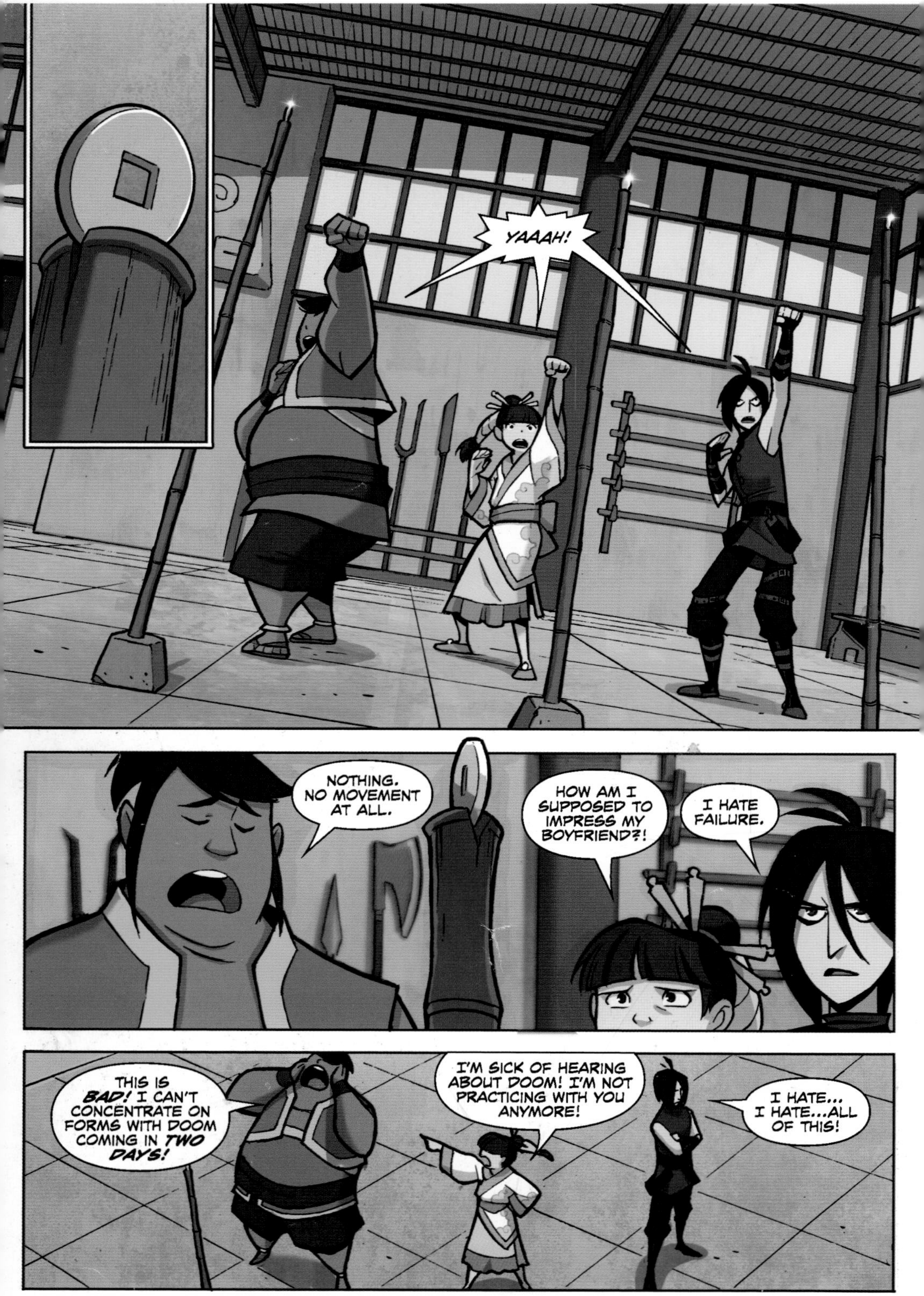
YAAAH!
NOTHING. NO MOVEMENT AT ALL.
HOW AM I SUPPOSED TO IMPRESS MY BOYFRIEND?!
I HATE FAILURE.
THIS IS BAD! I CAN'T CONCENTRATE ON FORMS WITH DOOM COMING IN TWO DAYS!
I'M SICK OF HEARING ABOUT DOOM! I'M NOT PRACTICING WITH YOU ANYMORE!
I HATE... I HATE...ALL OF THIS!

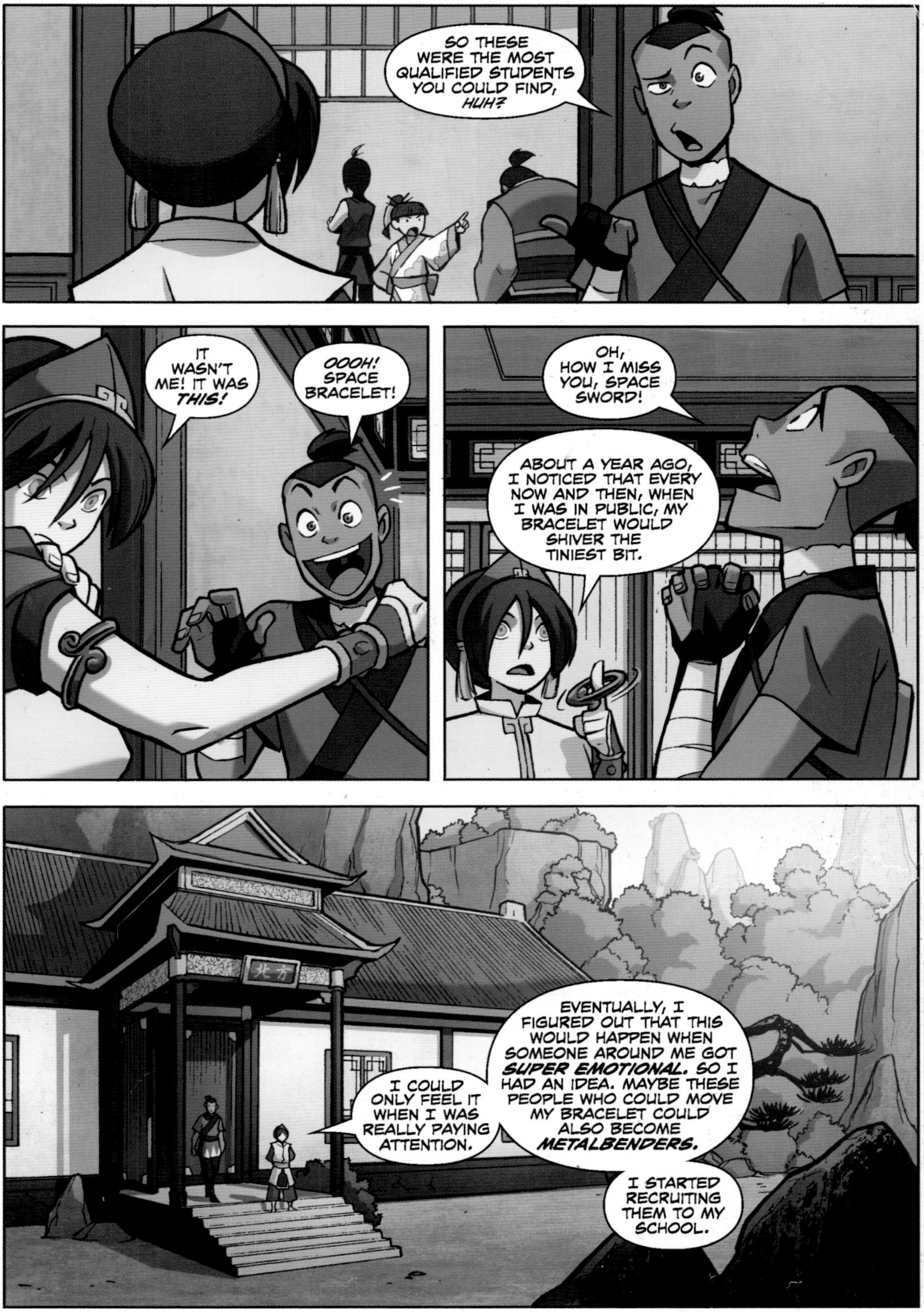
SO THESE WERE THE MOST QUALIFIED STUDENTS YOU COULD FIND, *HUH?*
IT WASN'T ME! IT WAS ***THIS!***
OOOH! SPACE BRACELET!
OH, HOW I MISS YOU, SPACE SWORD!
ABOUT A YEAR AGO, I NOTICED THAT EVERY NOW AND THEN, WHEN I WAS IN PUBLIC, MY BRACELET WOULD SHIVER THE TINIEST BIT.
I COULD ONLY FEEL IT WHEN I WAS REALLY PAYING ATTENTION.
EVENTUALLY, I FIGURED OUT THAT THIS WOULD HAPPEN WHEN SOMEONE AROUND ME GOT ***SUPER EMOTIONAL.*** SO I HAD AN IDEA. MAYBE THESE PEOPLE WHO COULD MOVE MY BRACELET COULD ALSO BECOME ***METALBENDERS.***
I STARTED RECRUITING THEM TO MY SCHOOL.

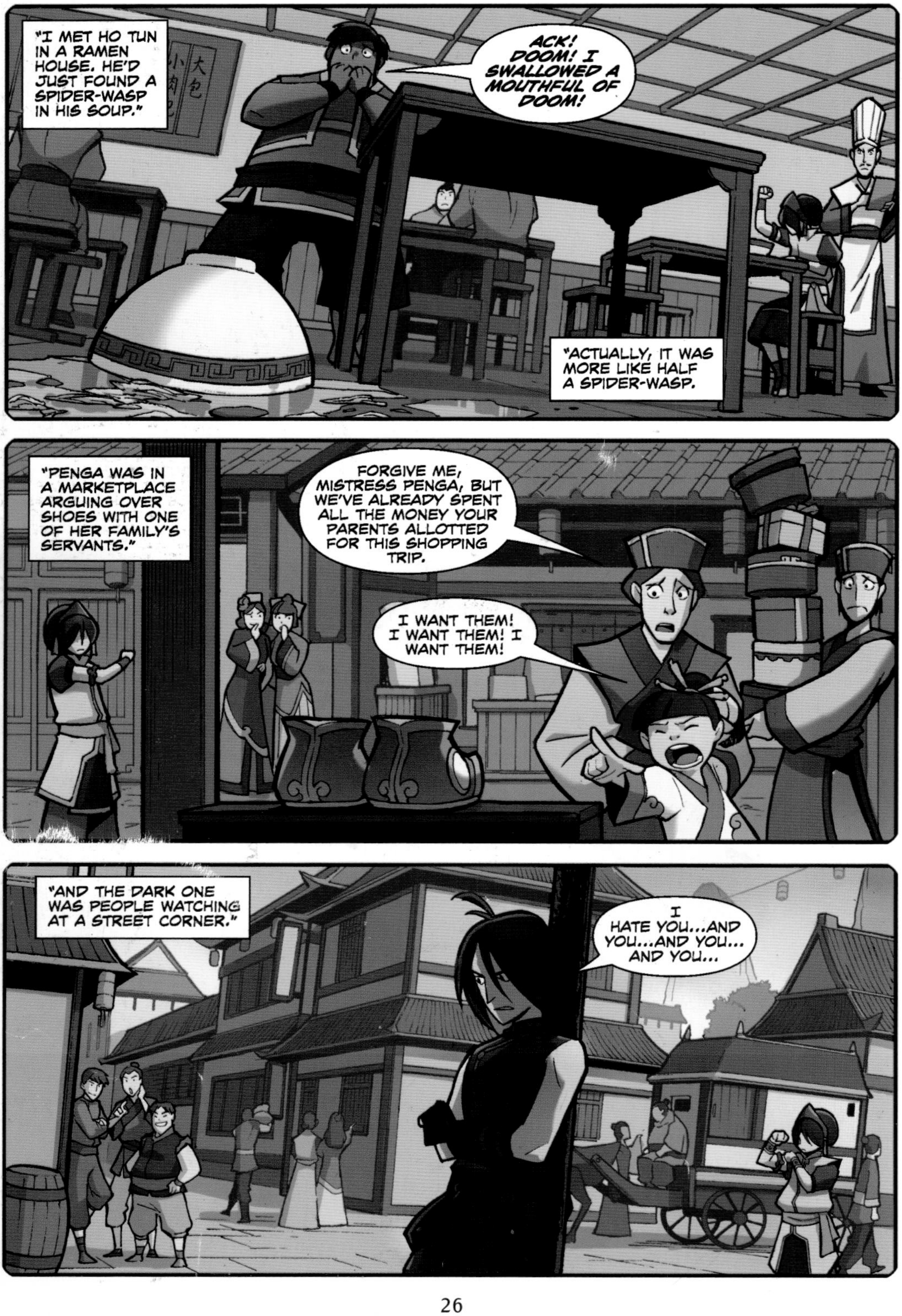
"I MET HO TUN IN A RAMEN HOUSE. HE'D JUST FOUND A SPIDER-WASP IN HIS SOUP."
ACK! DOOM! I SWALLOWED A MOUTHFUL OF DOOM!
"ACTUALLY, IT WAS MORE LIKE HALF A SPIDER-WASP.
"PENGA WAS IN A MARKETPLACE ARGUING OVER SHOES WITH ONE OF HER FAMILY'S SERVANTS."
FORGIVE ME, MISTRESS PENGA, BUT WE'VE ALREADY SPENT ALL THE MONEY YOUR PARENTS ALLOTTED FOR THIS SHOPPING TRIP.
I WANT THEM! I WANT THEM! I WANT THEM!
"AND THE DARK ONE WAS PEOPLE WATCHING AT A STREET CORNER."
I HATE YOU...AND YOU...AND YOU... AND YOU...

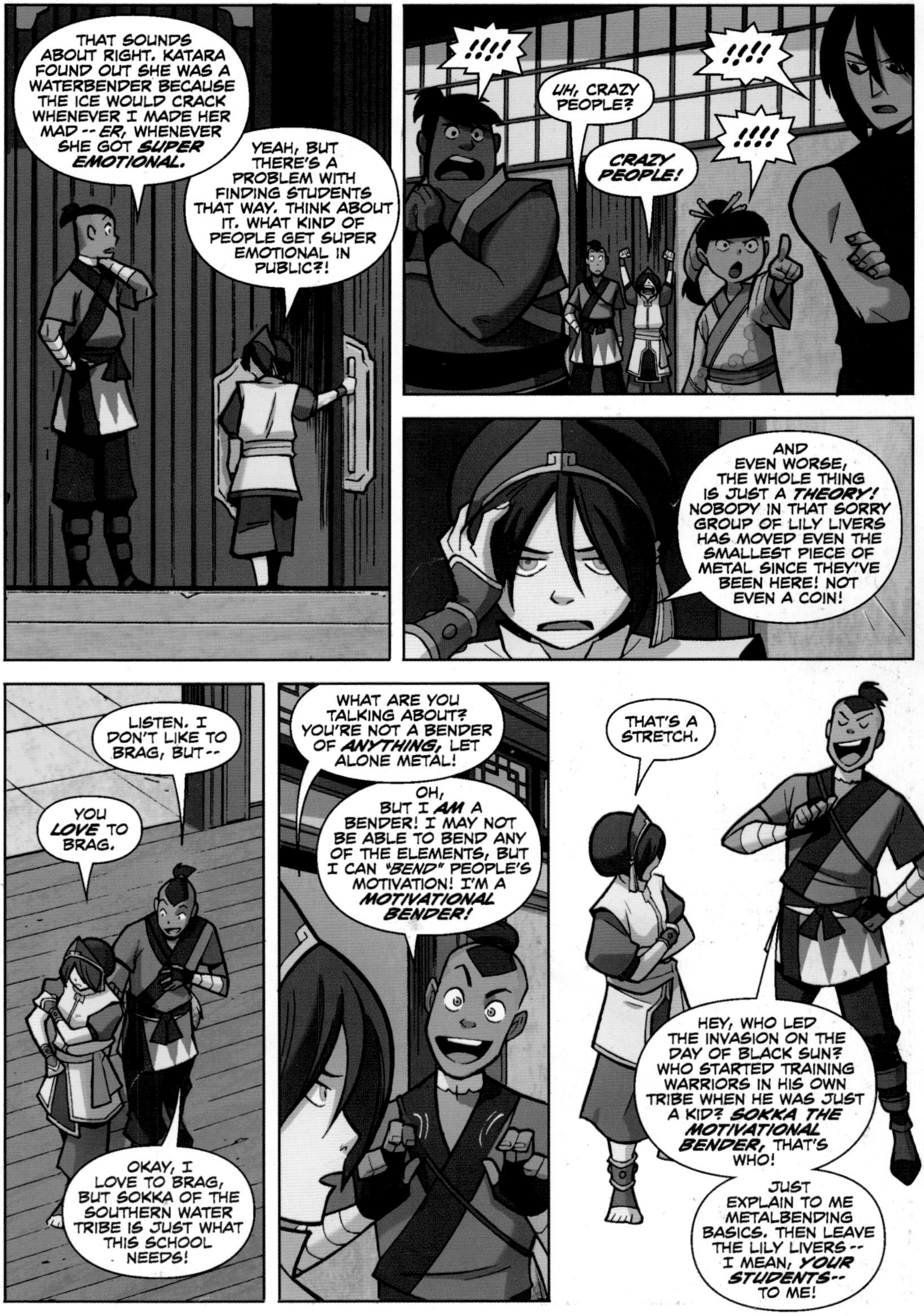

THAT SOUNDS ABOUT RIGHT. KATARA FOUND OUT SHE WAS A WATERBENDER BECAUSE THE ICE WOULD CRACK WHENEVER I MADE HER MAD -- *ER,* WHENEVER SHE GOT ***SUPER EMOTIONAL.***
YEAH, BUT THERE'S A PROBLEM WITH FINDING STUDENTS THAT WAY. THINK ABOUT IT. WHAT KIND OF PEOPLE GET SUPER EMOTIONAL IN PUBLIC?!
!!!!
UH, CRAZY PEOPLE?
CRAZY PEOPLE!
!!!!
!!!!
AND EVEN WORSE, THE WHOLE THING IS JUST A ***THEORY!*** NOBODY IN THAT SORRY GROUP OF LILY LIVERS HAS MOVED EVEN THE SMALLEST PIECE OF METAL SINCE THEY'VE BEEN HERE! NOT EVEN A COIN!
LISTEN. I DON'T LIKE TO BRAG, BUT --
YOU ***LOVE*** TO BRAG.
OKAY, I LOVE TO BRAG, BUT SOKKA OF THE SOUTHERN WATER TRIBE IS JUST WHAT THIS SCHOOL NEEDS!
WHAT ARE YOU TALKING ABOUT? YOU'RE NOT A BENDER OF ***ANYTHING,*** LET ALONE METAL!
OH, BUT I ***AM*** A BENDER! I MAY NOT BE ABLE TO BEND ANY OF THE ELEMENTS, BUT I CAN *"BEND"* PEOPLE'S MOTIVATION! I'M A ***MOTIVATIONAL BENDER!***
THAT'S A STRETCH.
HEY, WHO LED THE INVASION ON THE DAY OF BLACK SUN? WHO STARTED TRAINING WARRIORS IN HIS OWN TRIBE WHEN HE WAS JUST A KID? ***SOKKA THE MOTIVATIONAL BENDER,*** THAT'S WHO!
JUST EXPLAIN TO ME METALBENDING BASICS. THEN LEAVE THE LILY LIVERS -- I MEAN, ***YOUR STUDENTS --*** TO ME!

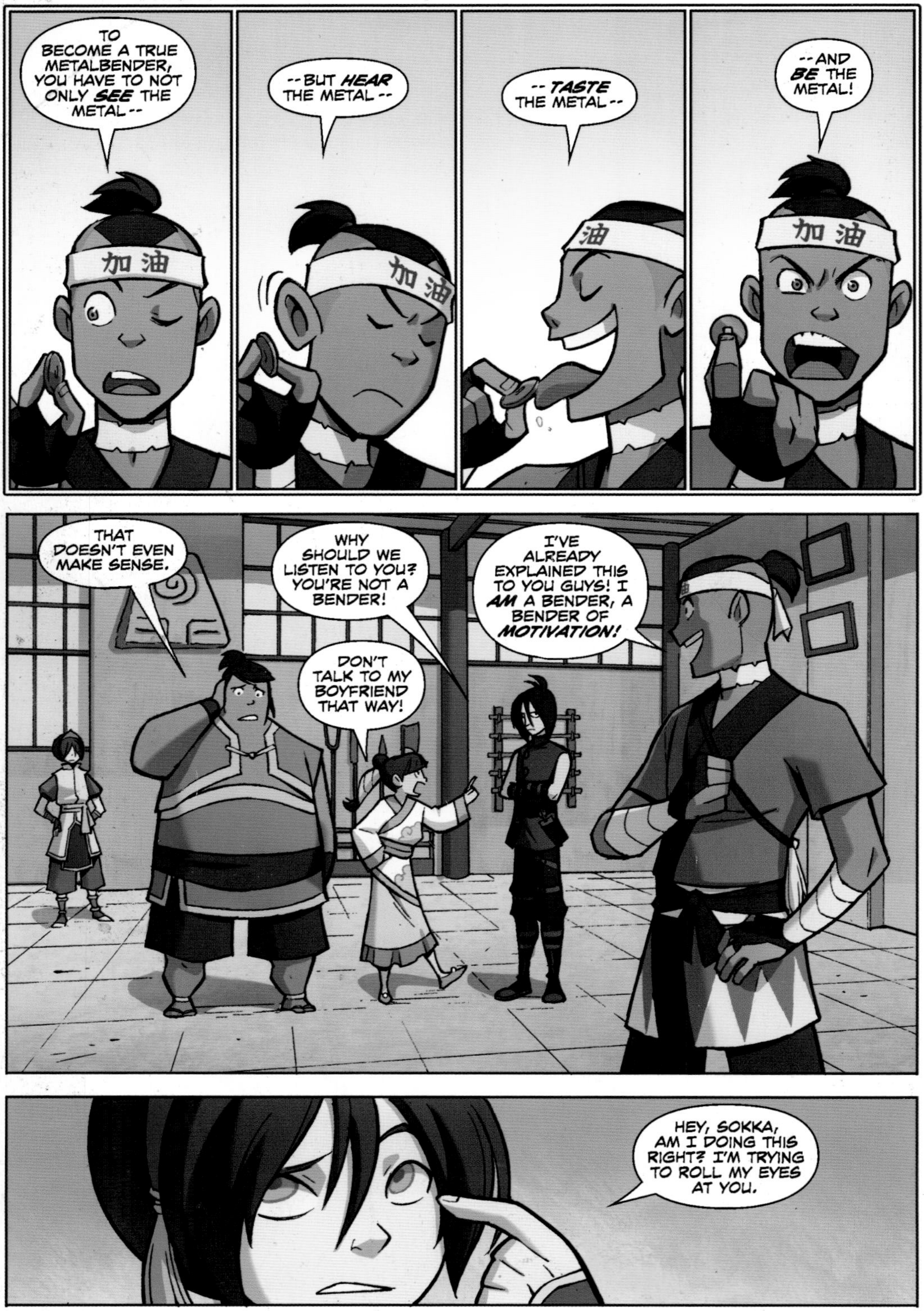
TO BECOME A TRUE METALBENDER, YOU HAVE TO NOT ONLY SEE THE METAL --
加油
-- BUT HEAR THE METAL --
加油
-- TASTE THE METAL --
油
-- AND BE THE METAL!
加油
THAT DOESN'T EVEN MAKE SENSE.
WHY SHOULD WE LISTEN TO YOU? YOU'RE NOT A BENDER!
DON'T TALK TO MY BOYFRIEND THAT WAY!
I'VE ALREADY EXPLAINED THIS TO YOU GUYS! I AM A BENDER, A BENDER OF MOTIVATION!
HEY, SOKKA, AM I DOING THIS RIGHT? I'M TRYING TO ROLL MY EYES AT YOU.

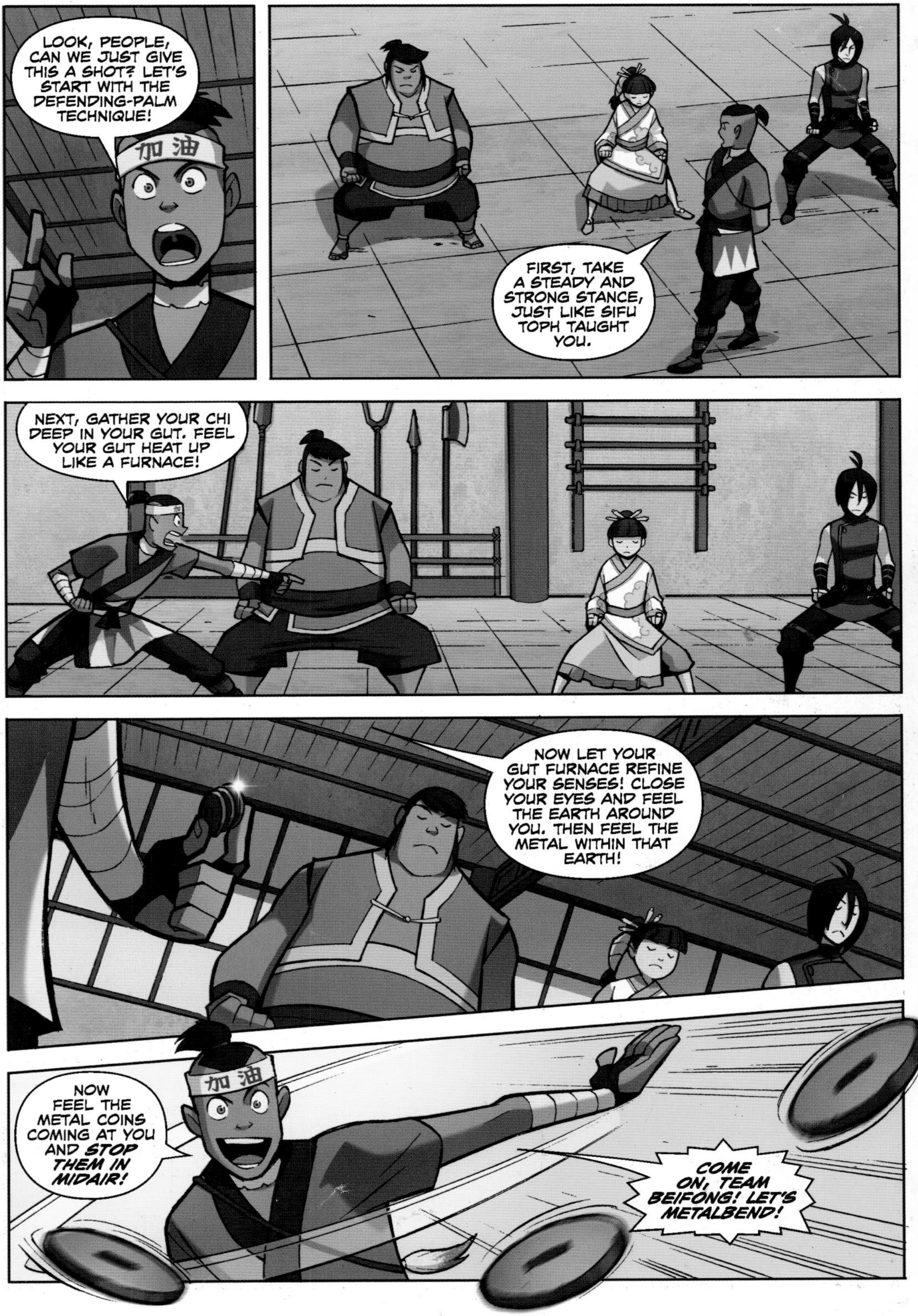

LOOK, PEOPLE, CAN WE JUST GIVE THIS A SHOT? LET'S START WITH THE DEFENDING-PALM TECHNIQUE!
加油
FIRST, TAKE A STEADY AND STRONG STANCE, JUST LIKE SIFU TOPH TAUGHT YOU.
NEXT, GATHER YOUR CHI DEEP IN YOUR GUT. FEEL YOUR GUT HEAT UP LIKE A FURNACE!
NOW LET YOUR GUT FURNACE REFINE YOUR SENSES! CLOSE YOUR EYES AND FEEL THE EARTH AROUND YOU. THEN FEEL THE METAL WITHIN THAT EARTH!
加油
NOW FEEL THE METAL COINS COMING AT YOU AND *STOP THEM IN MIDAIR!*
COME ON, TEAM BEIFONG! LET'S METALBEND!

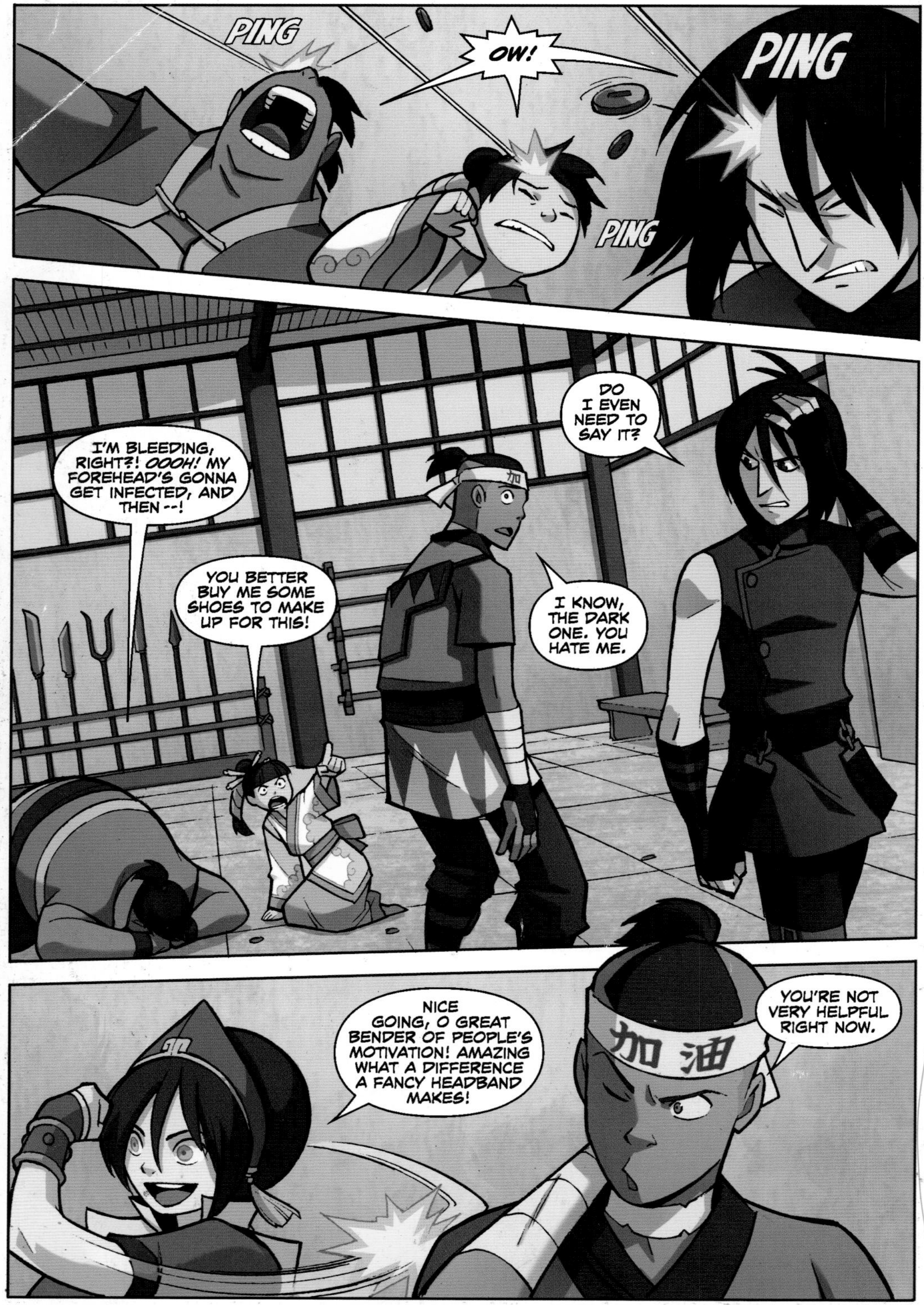
PING
OW!
PING
PING
DO I EVEN NEED TO SAY IT?
I'M BLEEDING, RIGHT?! OOOH! MY FOREHEAD'S GONNA GET INFECTED, AND THEN --!
YOU BETTER BUY ME SOME SHOES TO MAKE UP FOR THIS!
I KNOW, THE DARK ONE. YOU HATE ME.
NICE GOING, O GREAT BENDER OF PEOPLE'S MOTIVATION! AMAZING WHAT A DIFFERENCE A FANCY HEADBAND MAKES!
YOU'RE NOT VERY HELPFUL RIGHT NOW.
加油

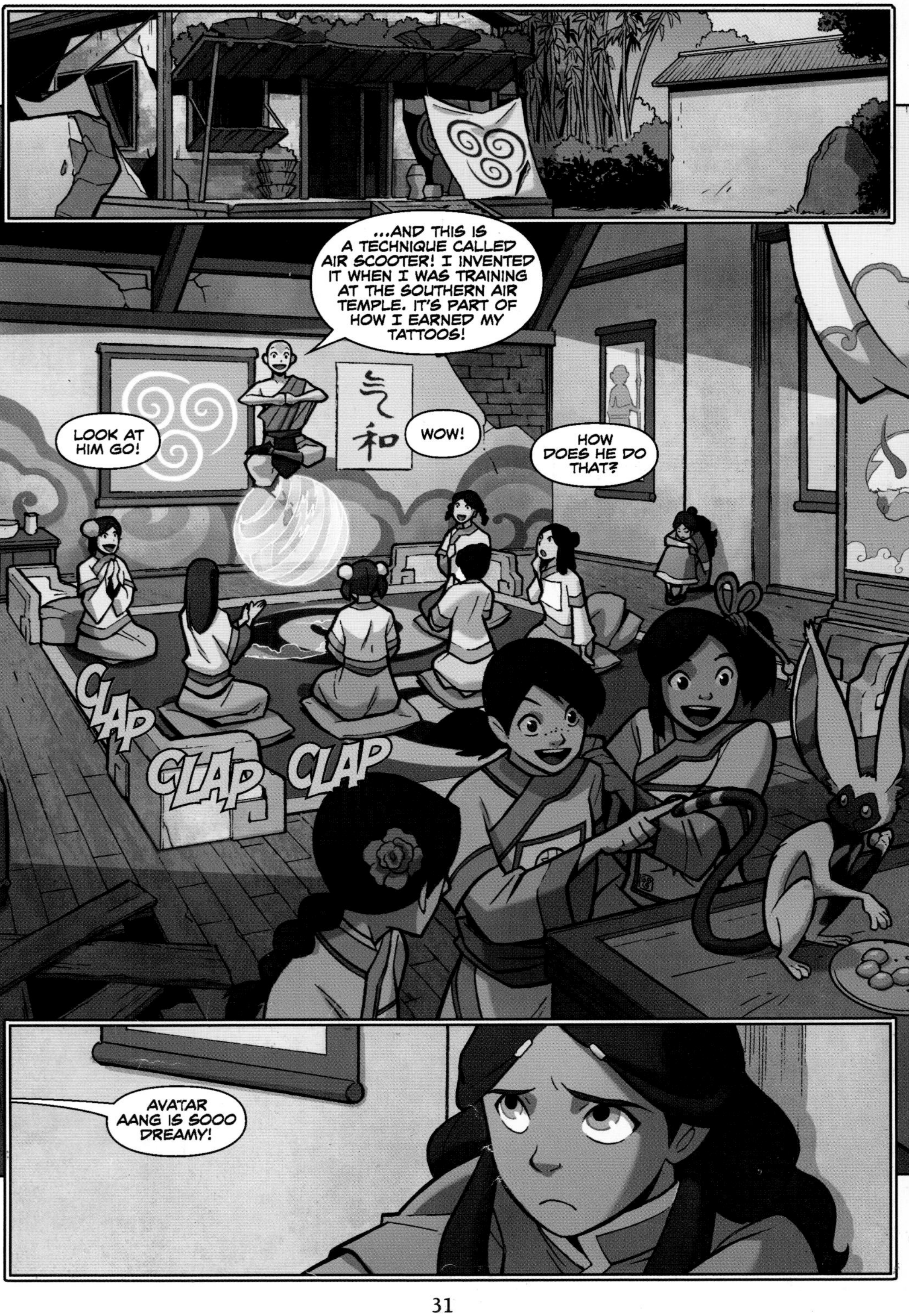
...AND THIS IS A TECHNIQUE CALLED AIR SCOOTER! I INVENTED IT WHEN I WAS TRAINING AT THE SOUTHERN AIR TEMPLE. IT'S PART OF HOW I EARNED MY TATTOOS!
LOOK AT HIM GO!
WOW!
HOW DOES HE DO THAT?
気
和
CLAP
CLAP
CLAP
AVATAR AANG IS SOOO DREAMY!

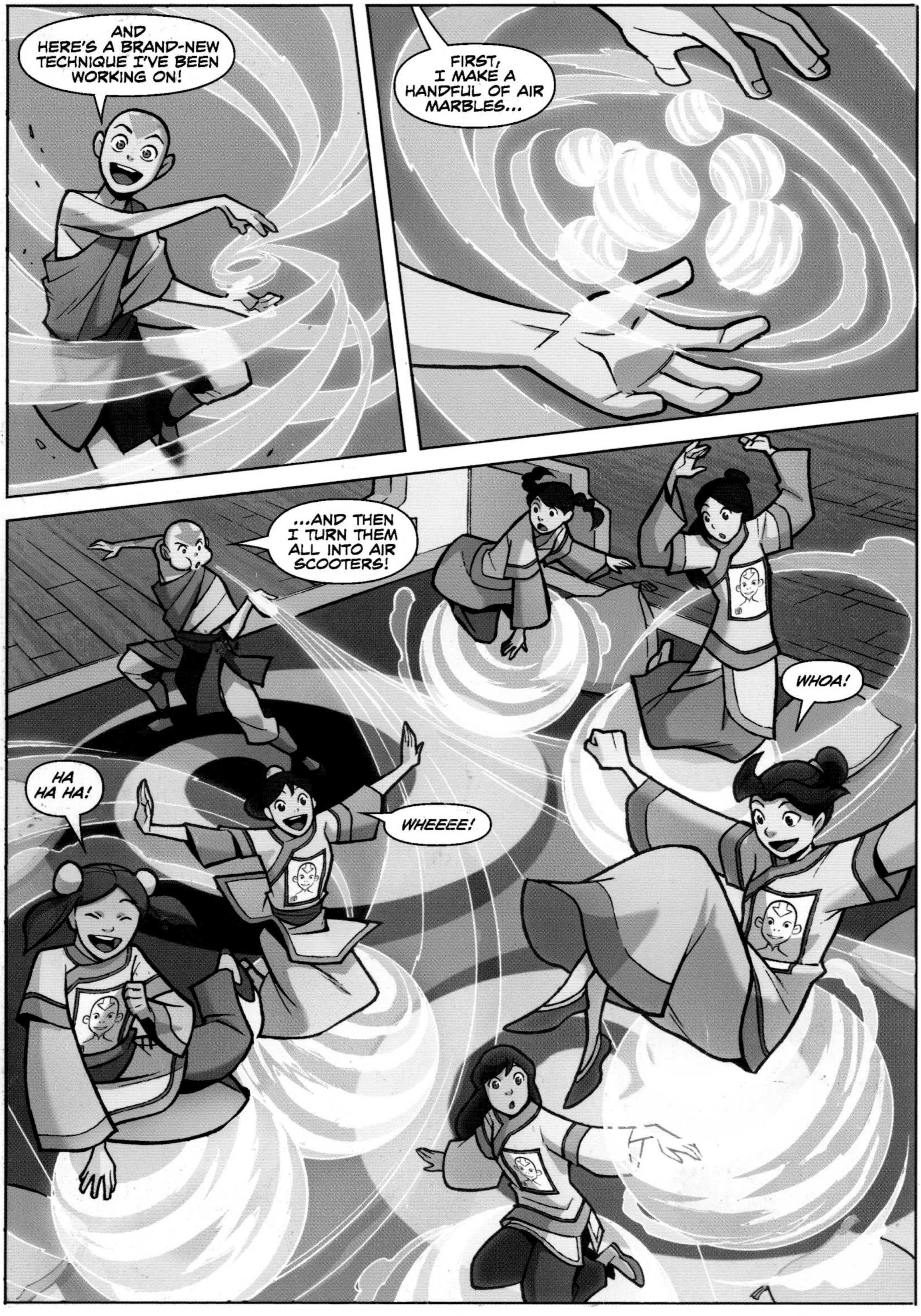
AND HERE'S A BRAND-NEW TECHNIQUE I'VE BEEN WORKING ON!
FIRST, I MAKE A HANDFUL OF AIR MARBLES...
...AND THEN I TURN THEM ALL INTO AIR SCOOTERS!
WHOA!
HA HA HA!
WHEEEE!

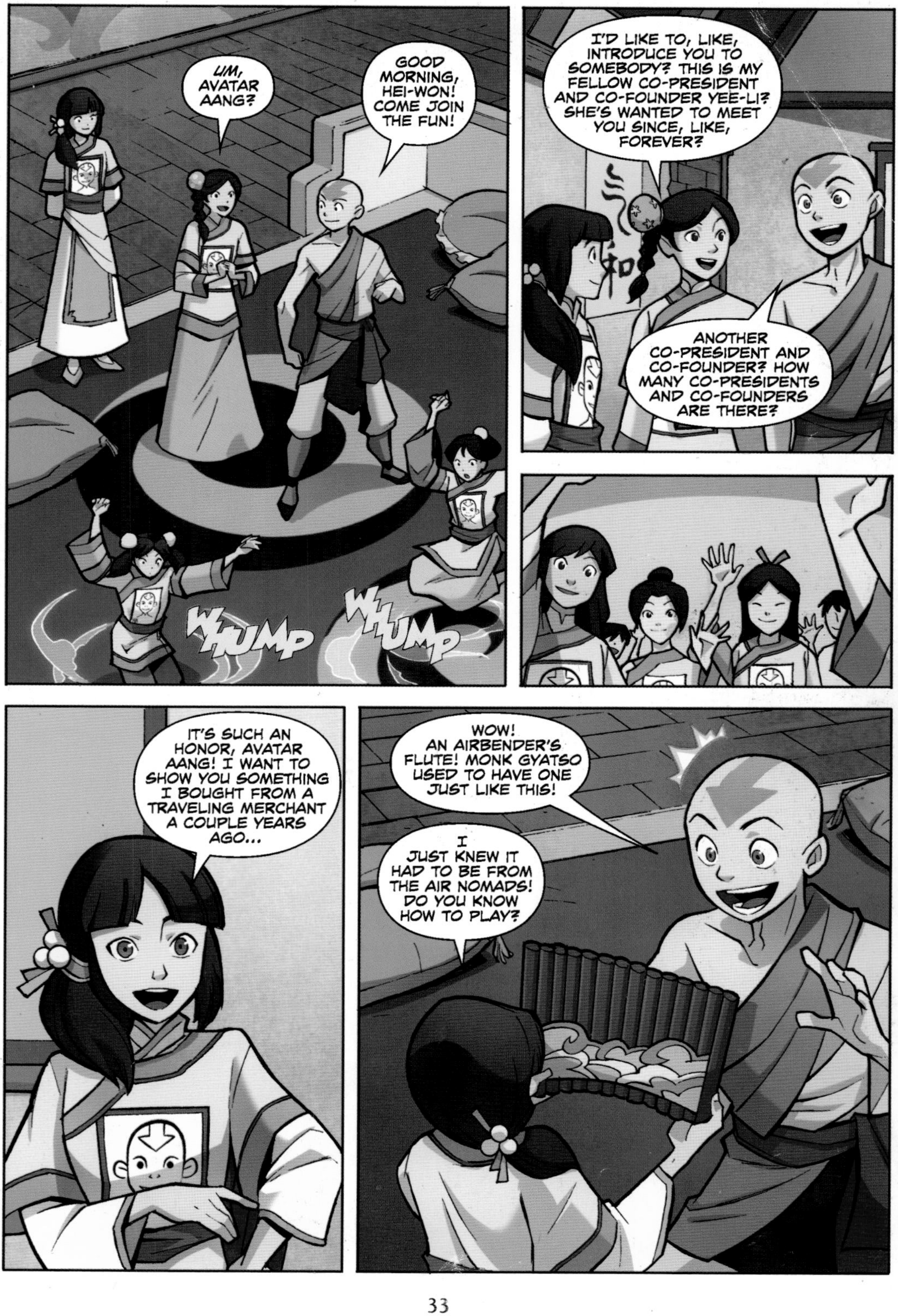
UM, AVATAR AANG?
GOOD MORNING, HEI-WON! COME JOIN THE FUN!
WHUMP
WHUMP
I'D LIKE TO, LIKE, INTRODUCE YOU TO SOMEBODY? THIS IS MY FELLOW CO-PRESIDENT AND CO-FOUNDER YEE-LI? SHE'S WANTED TO MEET YOU SINCE, LIKE, FOREVER?
ANOTHER CO-PRESIDENT AND CO-FOUNDER? HOW MANY CO-PRESIDENTS AND CO-FOUNDERS ARE THERE?
IT'S SUCH AN HONOR, AVATAR AANG! I WANT TO SHOW YOU SOMETHING I BOUGHT FROM A TRAVELING MERCHANT A COUPLE YEARS AGO...
WOW! AN AIRBENDER'S FLUTE! MONK GYATSO USED TO HAVE ONE JUST LIKE THIS!
I JUST KNEW IT HAD TO BE FROM THE AIR NOMADS! DO YOU KNOW HOW TO PLAY?

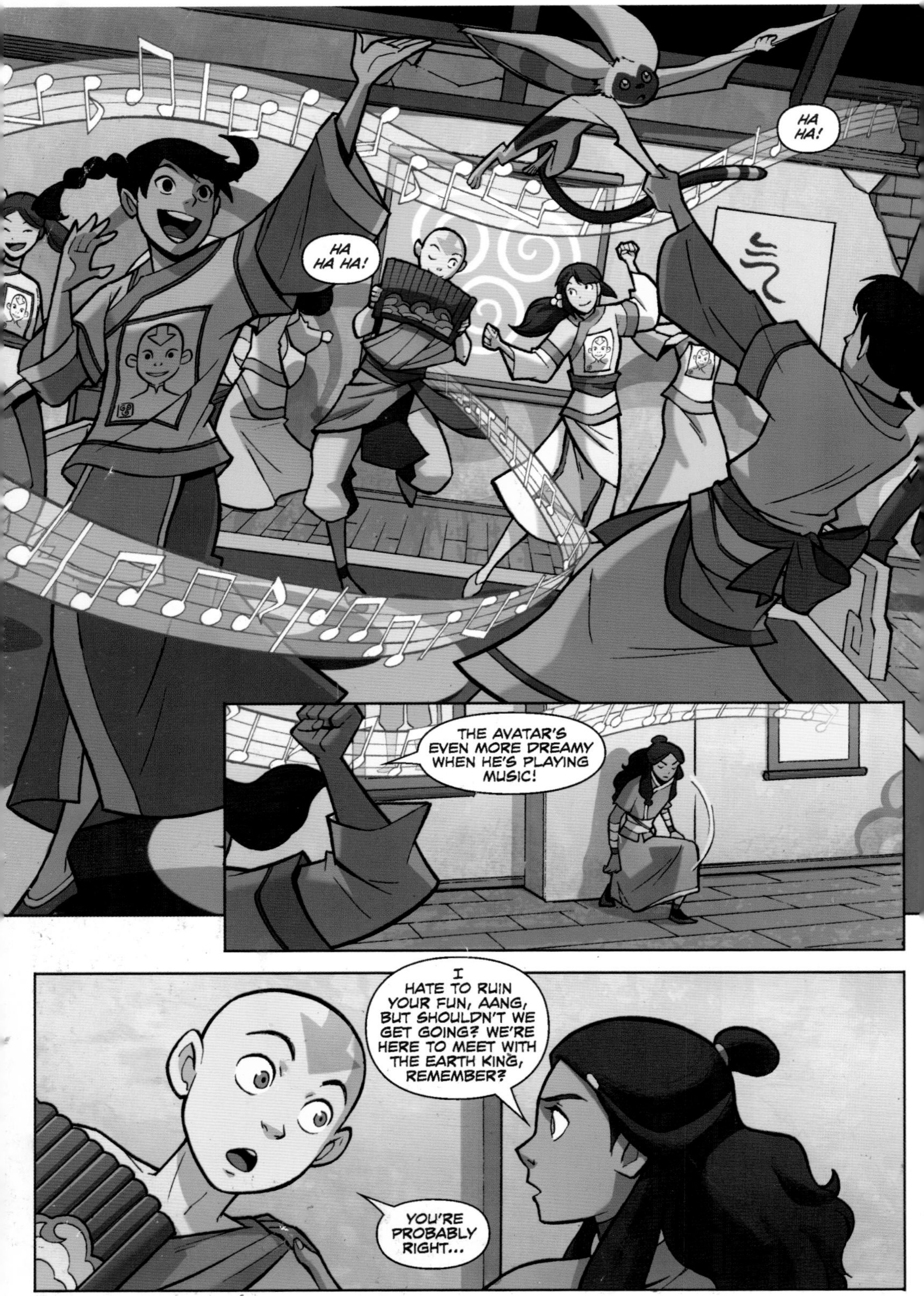
HA HA!
HA HA HA!
THE AVATAR'S EVEN MORE DREAMY WHEN HE'S PLAYING MUSIC!
I HATE TO RUIN YOUR FUN, AANG, BUT SHOULDN'T WE GET GOING? WE'RE HERE TO MEET WITH THE EARTH KING, REMEMBER?
YOU'RE PROBABLY RIGHT...

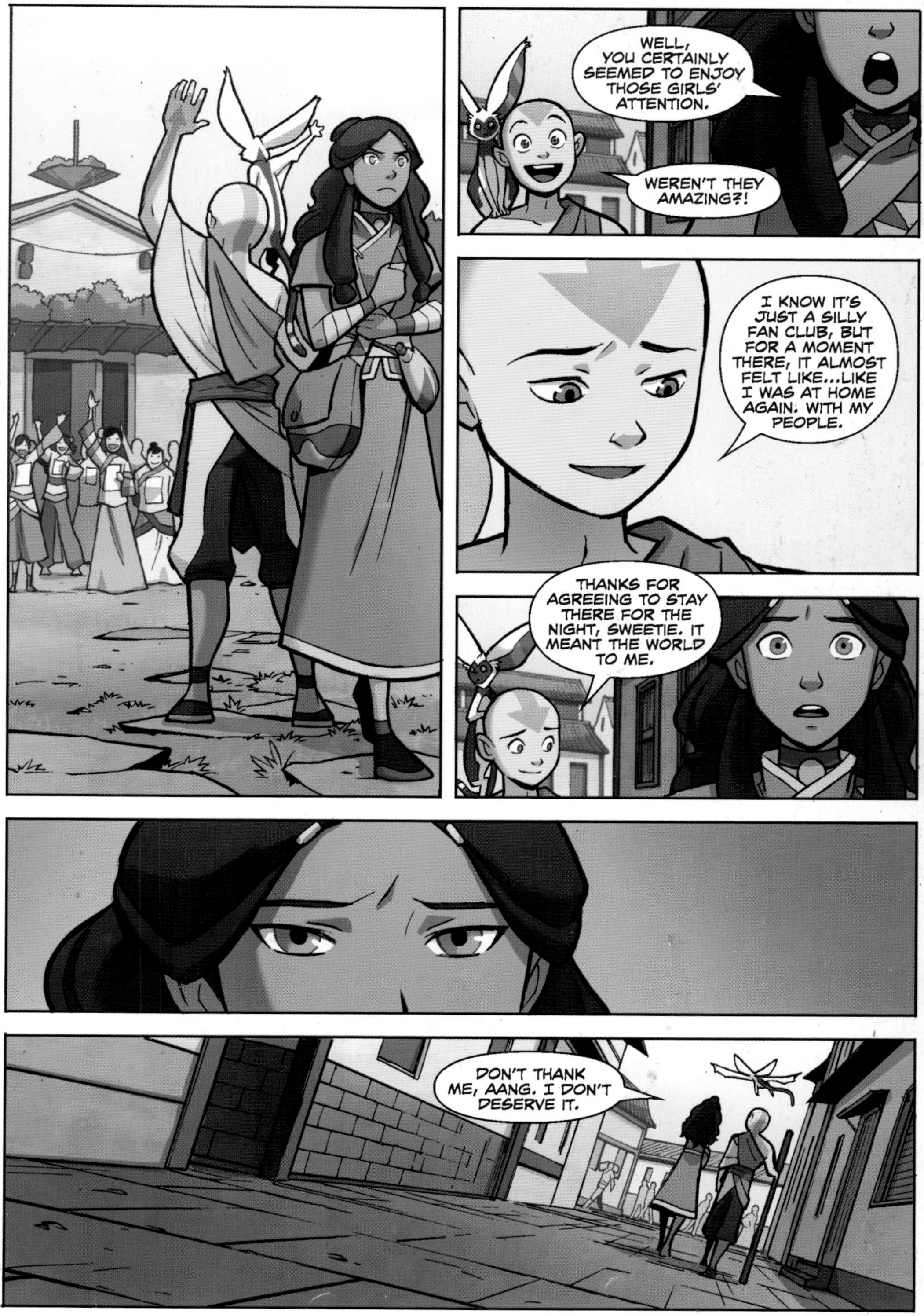
WELL, YOU CERTAINLY SEEMED TO ENJOY THOSE GIRLS' ATTENTION.
WEREN'T THEY AMAZING?!
I KNOW IT'S JUST A SILLY FAN CLUB, BUT FOR A MOMENT THERE, IT ALMOST FELT LIKE...LIKE I WAS AT HOME AGAIN. WITH MY PEOPLE.
THANKS FOR AGREEING TO STAY THERE FOR THE NIGHT, SWEETIE. IT MEANT THE WORLD TO ME.
DON'T THANK ME, AANG. I DON'T DESERVE IT.

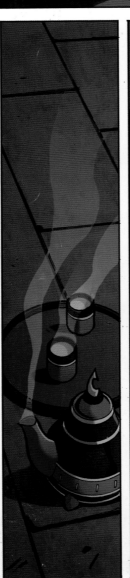

SIP

I STAYED UP ALL NIGHT THINKING ABOUT WHAT YOU SAID.

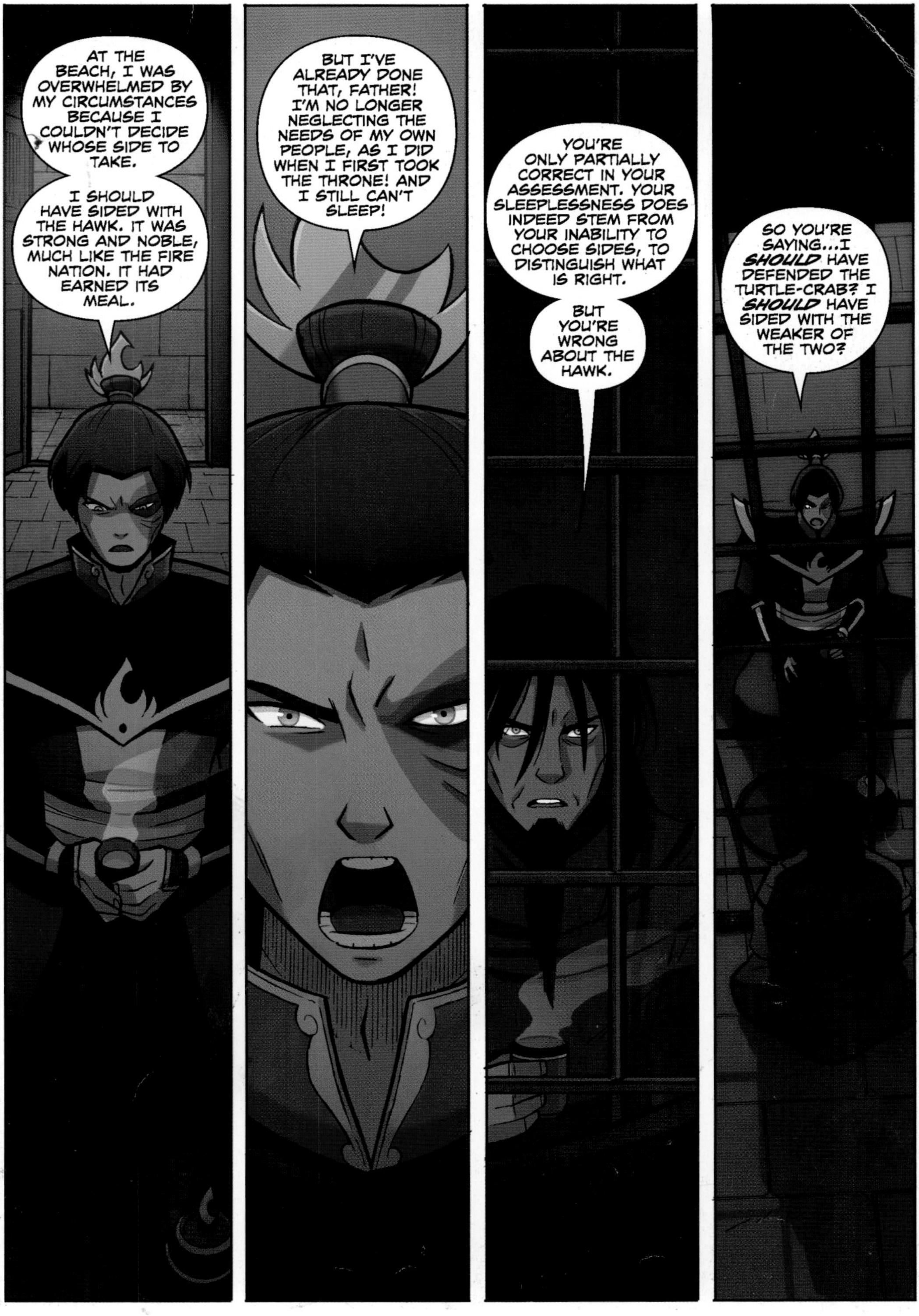
AT THE BEACH, I WAS OVERWHELMED BY MY CIRCUMSTANCES BECAUSE I COULDN'T DECIDE WHOSE SIDE TO TAKE.
I SHOULD HAVE SIDED WITH THE HAWK. IT WAS STRONG AND NOBLE, MUCH LIKE THE FIRE NATION. IT HAD EARNED ITS MEAL.
BUT I'VE ALREADY DONE THAT, FATHER! I'M NO LONGER NEGLECTING THE NEEDS OF MY OWN PEOPLE, AS I DID WHEN I FIRST TOOK THE THRONE! AND I STILL CAN'T SLEEP!
YOU'RE ONLY PARTIALLY CORRECT IN YOUR ASSESSMENT. YOUR SLEEPLESSNESS DOES INDEED STEM FROM YOUR INABILITY TO CHOOSE SIDES, TO DISTINGUISH WHAT IS RIGHT.
BUT YOU'RE WRONG ABOUT THE HAWK.
SO YOU'RE SAYING...I *SHOULD* HAVE DEFENDED THE TURTLE-CRAB? I *SHOULD* HAVE SIDED WITH THE WEAKER OF THE TWO?

WHAT I'M SAYING IS THIS -- *THERE IS NO RIGHT OR WRONG APART FROM WHAT YOU DECIDE.* WHO YOU CHOOSE TO DEFEND DESERVES TO BE DEFENDED SIMPLY BECAUSE *YOU* CHOSE THEM.

YOU ARE THE *FIRE LORD.*

WHAT YOU CHOOSE, BY DEFINITION, IS *RIGHT.*

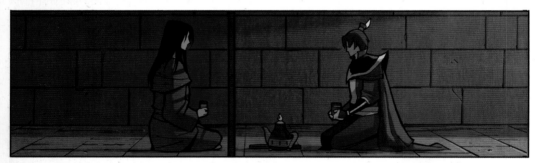

NO! RIGHT AND WRONG ARE BIGGER THAN *ME,* OR *YOU,* OR EVEN *THE AVATAR!*

AND I BELIEVE THAT THE AVATAR, THE EARTH KING, AND I CAN COME CLOSEST TO WHAT'S RIGHT BY WORKING *TOGETHER!*

I'VE HEARD RUMORS ABOUT THIS LITTLE MEETING OF YOURS.

DO YOU THINK THE EARTH KING, AFTER BEING HUMILIATED TIME AND TIME AGAIN BY OUR MIGHTY NATION AND HIS OWN INCOMPETENCE, WILL BE *REASONABLE?* DO YOU THINK HE'LL TREAT THE REMAINING FIRE NATION COLONIALS *FAIRLY?*

IN AN ATTEMPT TO RESTORE HIS OWN DIGNITY, HE'LL SEND OUT HIS ARMY TO CRUSH THEM!

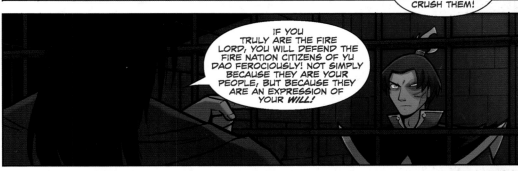

IF YOU TRULY ARE THE FIRE LORD, YOU WILL DEFEND THE FIRE NATION CITIZENS OF YU DAO FEROCIOUSLY! NOT SIMPLY BECAUSE THEY ARE YOUR PEOPLE, BUT BECAUSE THEY ARE AN EXPRESSION OF YOUR *WILL!*

I'M GOING TO *WAIT,* AND MY PATIENCE WILL BE REWARDED WITH A PEACEFUL RESOLUTION FOR EVERYONE! EVEN AS WE SPEAK, THE AVATAR IS --

THE AVATAR IS AN IRRELEVANT RELIC OF A BYGONE AGE! HE WANTS TO KEEP THE WORLD FROZEN IN TIME BY DENYING THE INEVITABLE VICTORY OF THE STRONG OVER THE WEAK!

AVATAR AANG IS MY FRIEND! MORE OFTEN THAN NOT, HE'S BEEN ON THE SIDE THAT'S *RIGHT!* I TRUST HIM.

MORE THAN YOU TRUST YOURSELF?

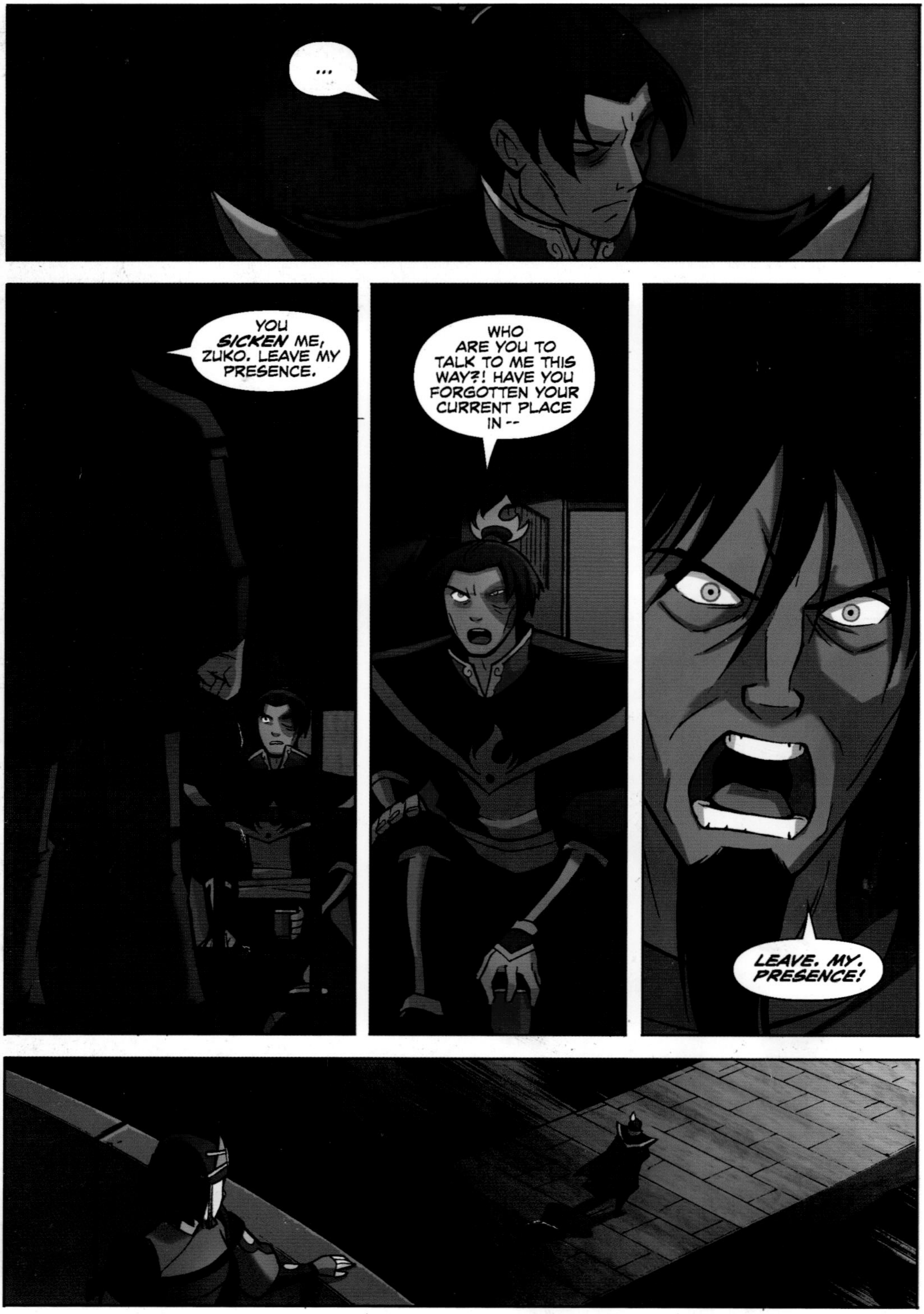
...
YOU SICKEN ME, ZUKO. LEAVE MY PRESENCE.
WHO ARE YOU TO TALK TO ME THIS WAY?! HAVE YOU FORGOTTEN YOUR CURRENT PLACE IN --
LEAVE. MY. PRESENCE!

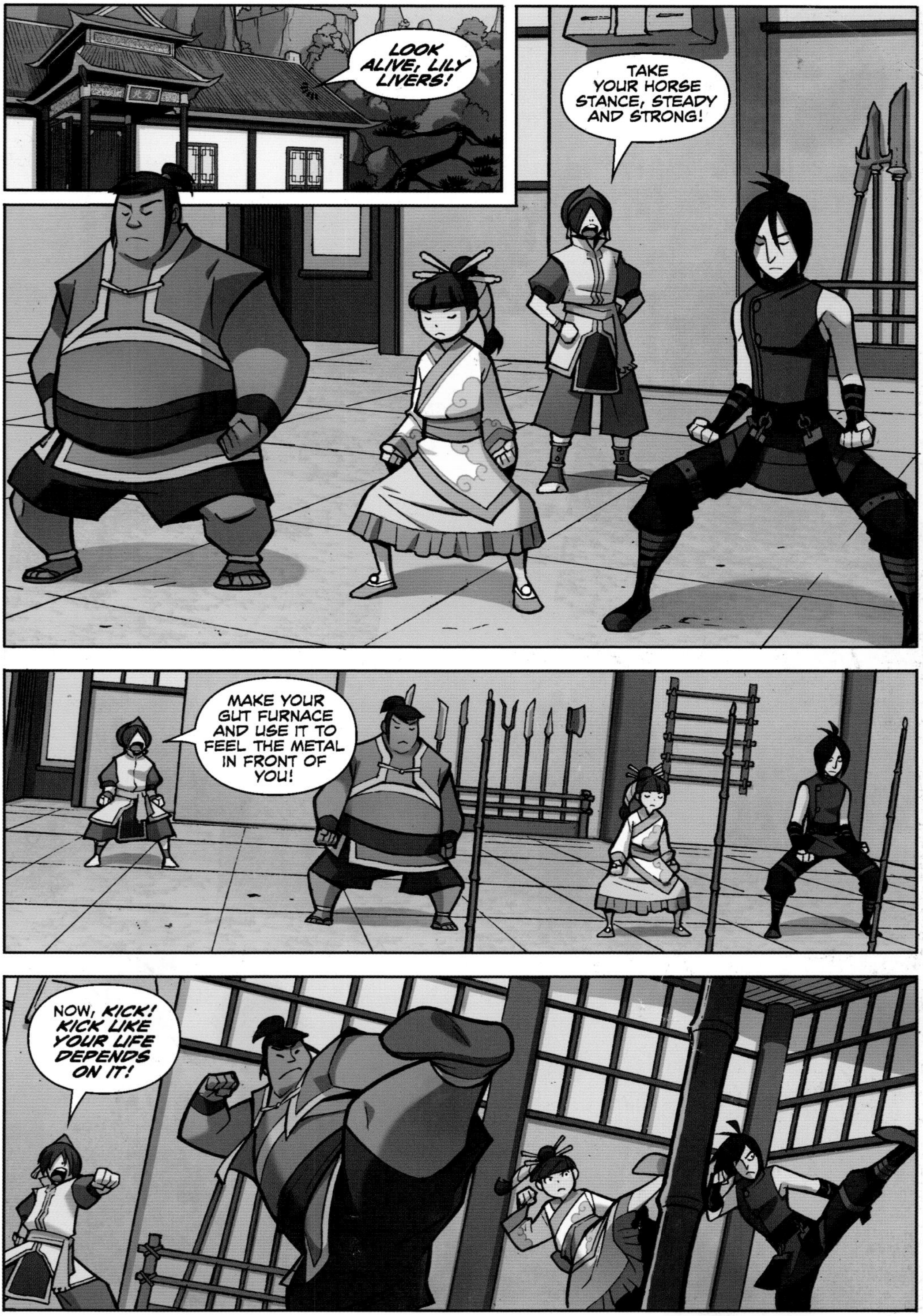
LOOK ALIVE, LILY LIVERS!
TAKE YOUR HORSE STANCE, STEADY AND STRONG!
MAKE YOUR GUT FURNACE AND USE IT TO FEEL THE METAL IN FRONT OF YOU!
NOW, KICK! KICK LIKE YOUR LIFE DEPENDS ON IT!

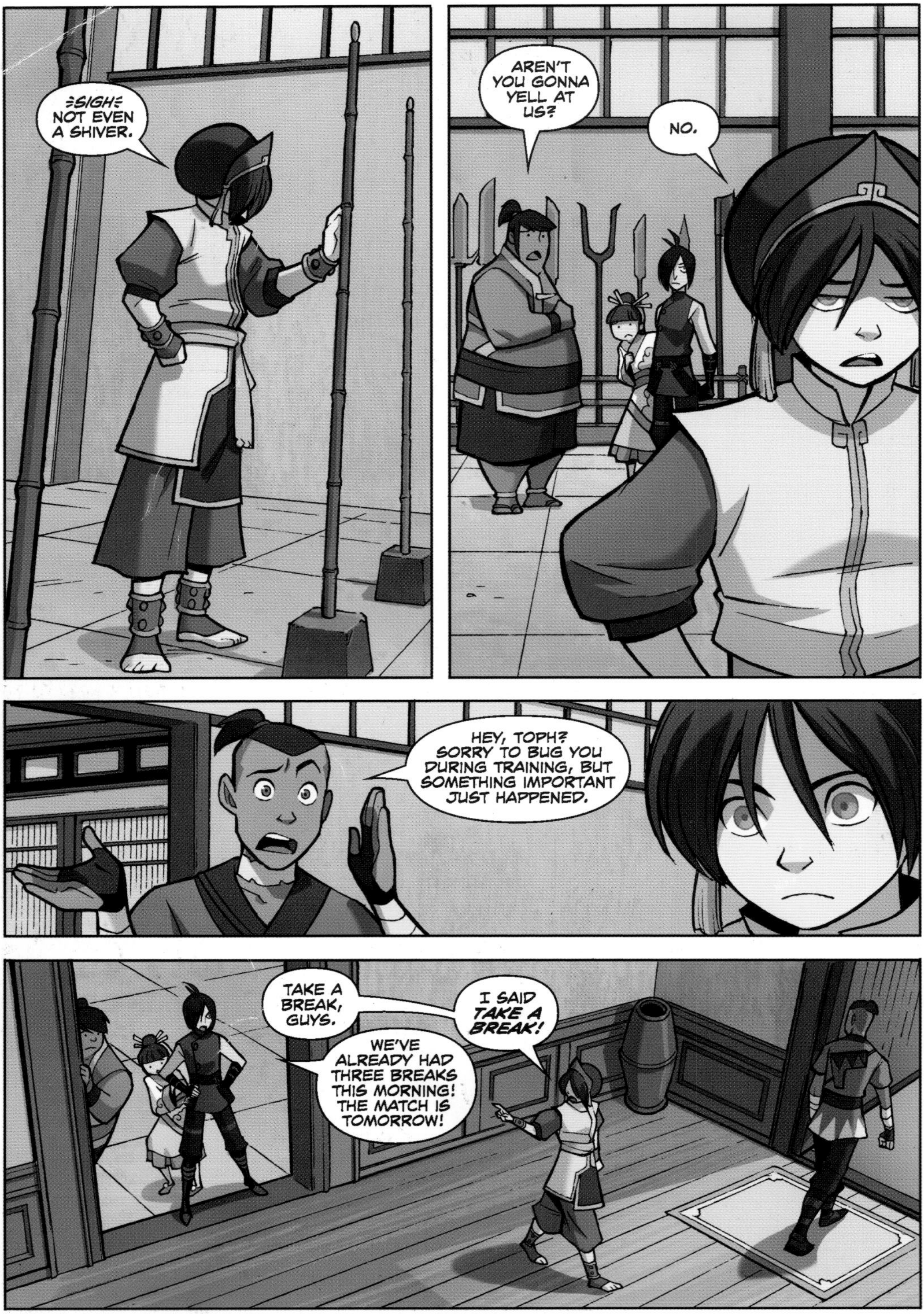

≈SIGH≈ NOT EVEN A SHIVER.
AREN'T YOU GONNA YELL AT US?
NO.
HEY, TOPH? SORRY TO BUG YOU DURING TRAINING, BUT SOMETHING IMPORTANT JUST HAPPENED.
TAKE A BREAK, GUYS.
WE'VE ALREADY HAD THREE BREAKS THIS MORNING! THE MATCH IS TOMORROW!
I SAID *TAKE A BREAK!*

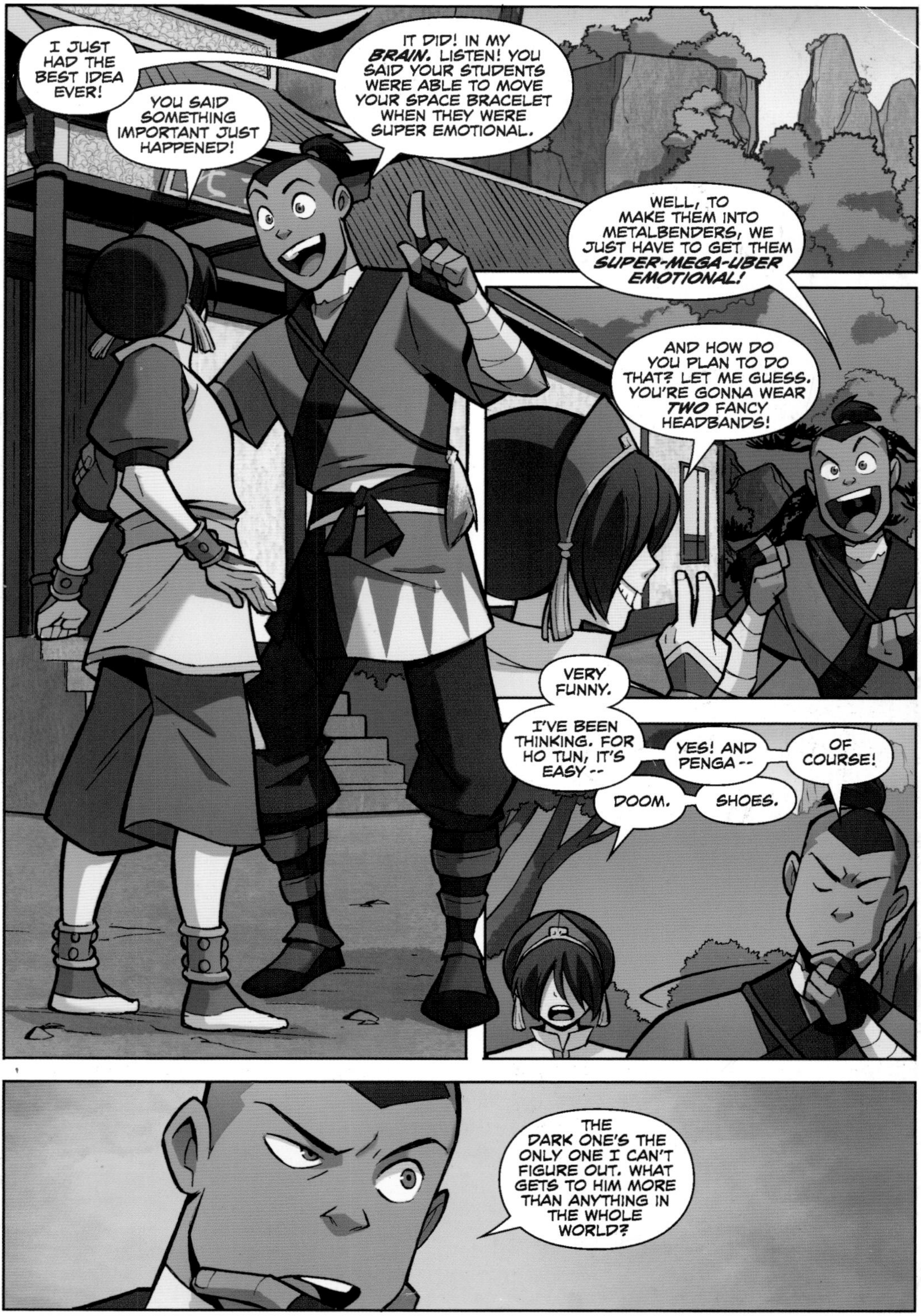

I JUST HAD THE BEST IDEA EVER!
YOU SAID SOMETHING IMPORTANT JUST HAPPENED!
IT DID! IN MY BRAIN. LISTEN! YOU SAID YOUR STUDENTS WERE ABLE TO MOVE YOUR SPACE BRACELET WHEN THEY WERE SUPER EMOTIONAL.
WELL, TO MAKE THEM INTO METALBENDERS, WE JUST HAVE TO GET THEM SUPER-MEGA-UBER EMOTIONAL!
AND HOW DO YOU PLAN TO DO THAT? LET ME GUESS. YOU'RE GONNA WEAR TWO FANCY HEADBANDS!
VERY FUNNY.
I'VE BEEN THINKING. FOR HO TUN, IT'S EASY --
DOOM.
YES! AND PENGA --
SHOES.
OF COURSE!
THE DARK ONE'S THE ONLY ONE I CAN'T FIGURE OUT. WHAT GETS TO HIM MORE THAN ANYTHING IN THE WHOLE WORLD?

HIS REAL NAME. BUT I PROMISED I WOULDN'T EVER TELL ANYBODY.

PLEASE PLEASEPLEASEPLEASE PLEASE--

OKAY, OKAY! QUIT YOUR BLUBBERING!

NO. WAY. WHAT WERE HIS PARENTS THINKING?

I KNOW, RIGHT? NO WONDER THAT GUY HATES EVERYTHING!

NOW, YOU REMEMBER WHAT YOU DID DURING OUR FINAL BATTLE WITH OZAI? IN THE CABIN OF THAT FIRE NATION AIRSHIP? I NEED YOU TO DO SOMETHING LIKE THAT! IF ONLY WE HAD A WHOLE BUNCH OF METAL TO WORK WITH...

WHY DIDN'T YOU SAY SO? THERE'S A BUNKER FULL OF METAL UNDER THE SCHOOL BUILDING!

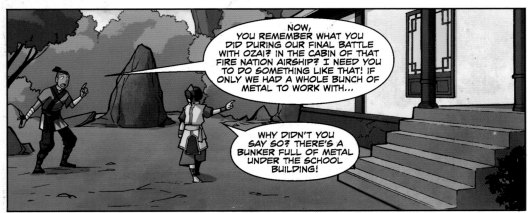

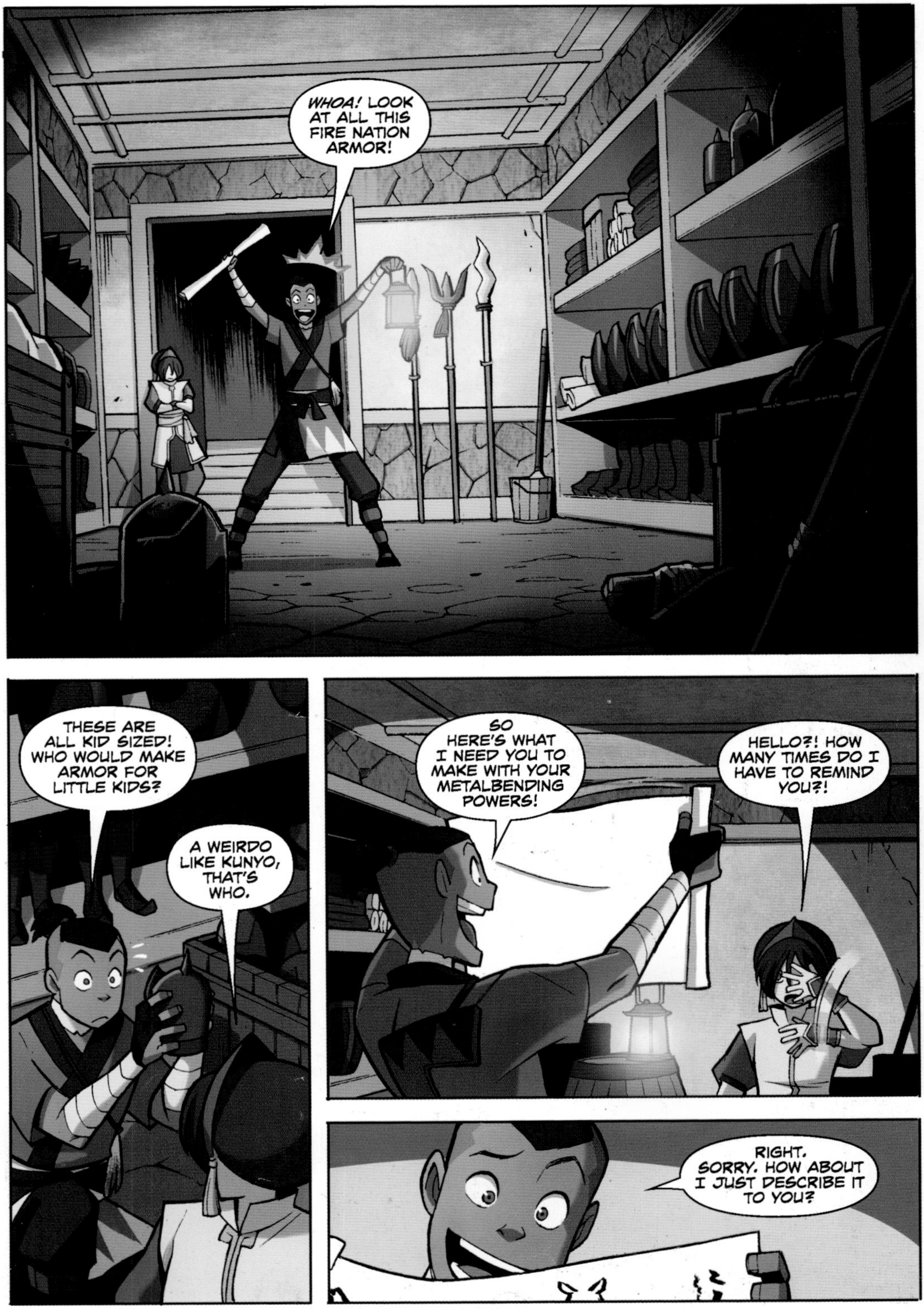
WHOA! LOOK AT ALL THIS FIRE NATION ARMOR!
THESE ARE ALL KID SIZED! WHO WOULD MAKE ARMOR FOR LITTLE KIDS?
A WEIRDO LIKE KUNYO, THAT'S WHO.
SO HERE'S WHAT I NEED YOU TO MAKE WITH YOUR METALBENDING POWERS!
HELLO?! HOW MANY TIMES DO I HAVE TO REMIND YOU?!
RIGHT. SORRY. HOW ABOUT I JUST DESCRIBE IT TO YOU?

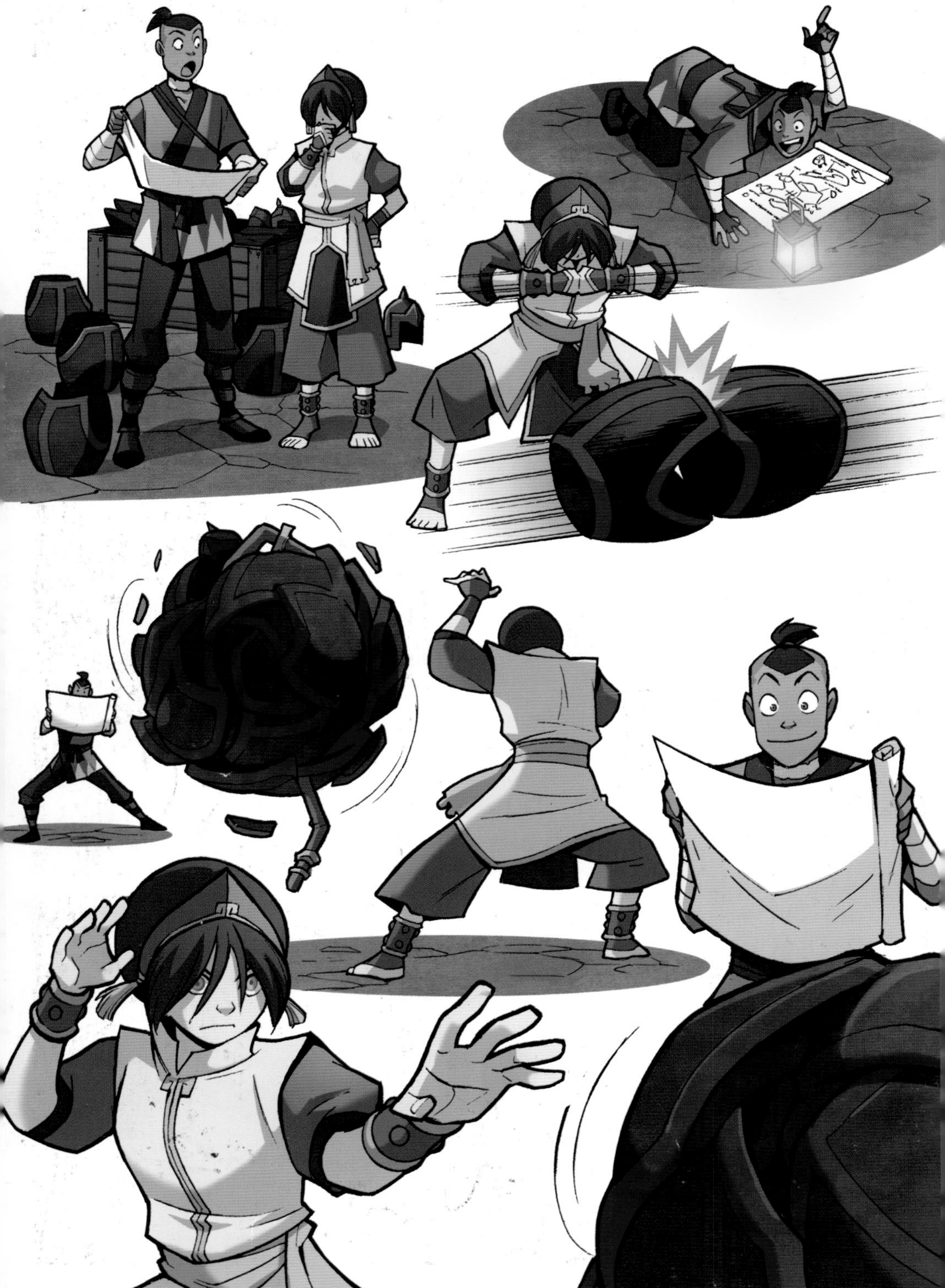

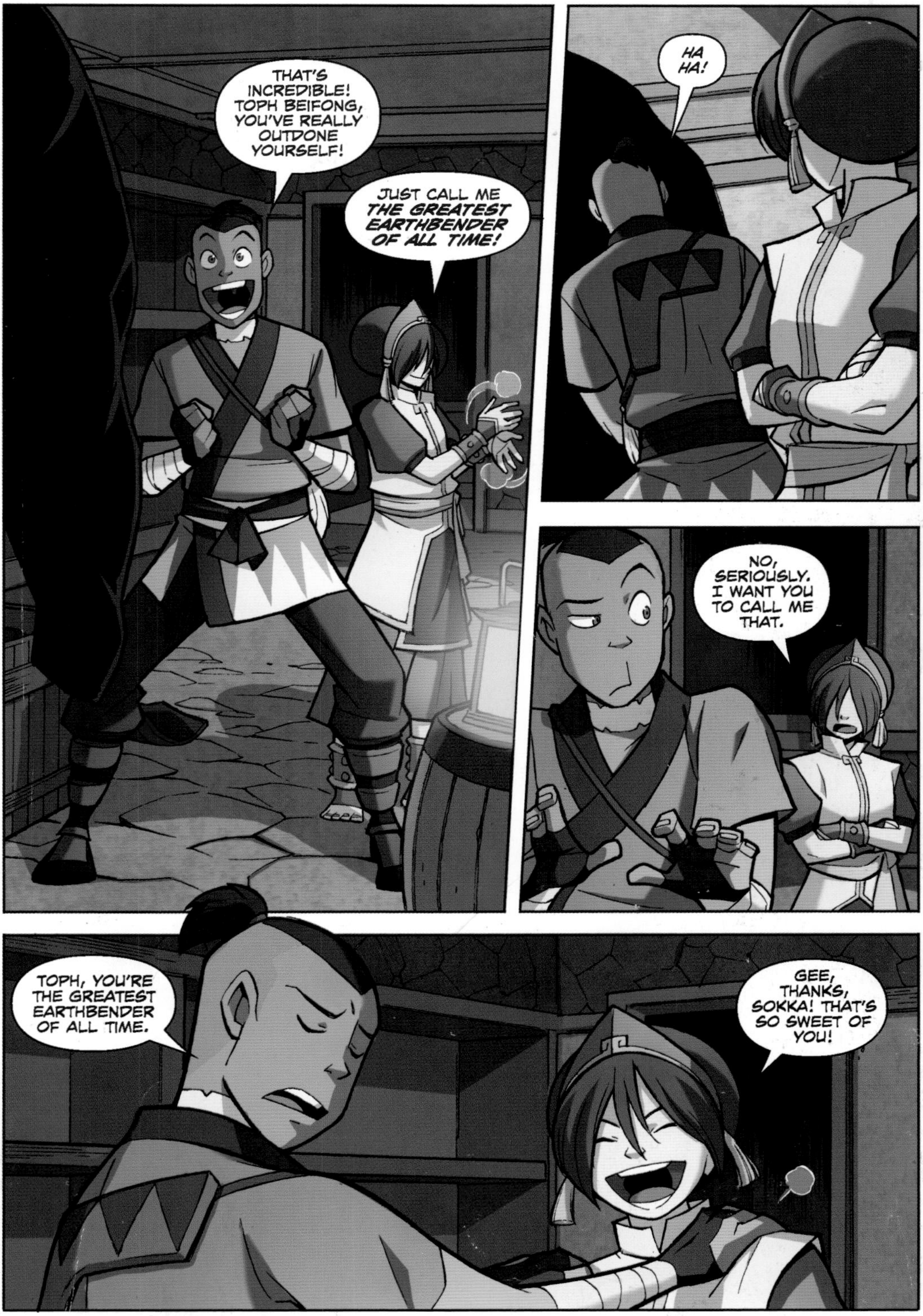
THAT'S INCREDIBLE! TOPH BEIFONG, YOU'VE REALLY OUTDONE YOURSELF!
JUST CALL ME *THE GREATEST EARTHBENDER OF ALL TIME!*
HA HA!
NO, SERIOUSLY. I WANT YOU TO CALL ME THAT.
TOPH, YOU'RE THE GREATEST EARTHBENDER OF ALL TIME.
GEE, THANKS, SOKKA! THAT'S SO SWEET OF YOU!

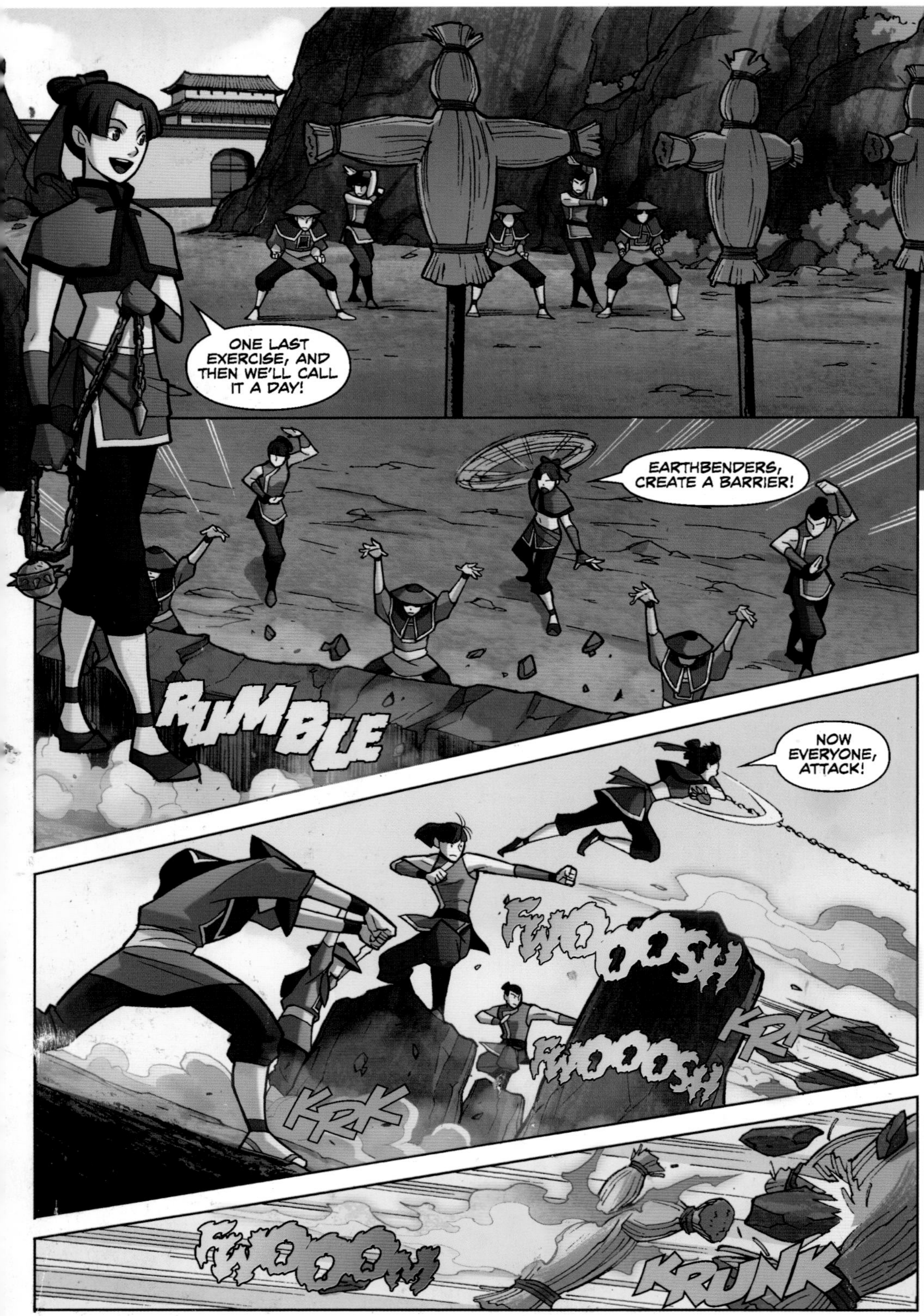
ONE LAST EXERCISE, AND THEN WE'LL CALL IT A DAY!
EARTHBENDERS, CREATE A BARRIER!
RUMBLE
NOW EVERYONE, ATTACK!
FWOOOSH
KRK
FWOOOSH
KRK
FWOOOM
KRUNK

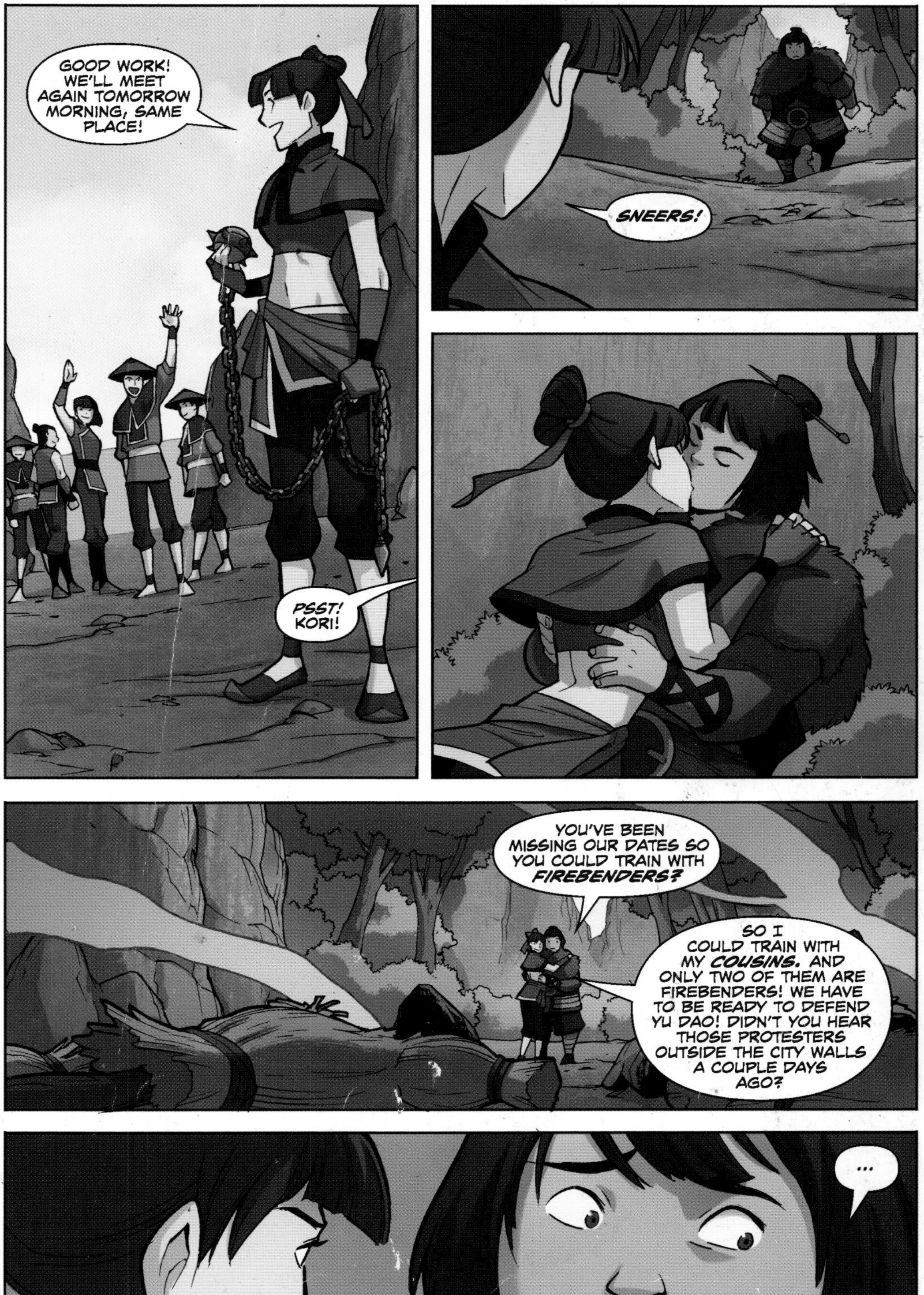
GOOD WORK! WE'LL MEET AGAIN TOMORROW MORNING, SAME PLACE!
PSST! KORI!
SNEERS!
YOU'VE BEEN MISSING OUR DATES SO YOU COULD TRAIN WITH *FIREBENDERS?*
SO I COULD TRAIN WITH MY *COUSINS.* AND ONLY TWO OF THEM ARE FIREBENDERS! WE HAVE TO BE READY TO DEFEND YU DAO! DIDN'T YOU HEAR THOSE PROTESTERS OUTSIDE THE CITY WALLS A COUPLE DAYS AGO?
...

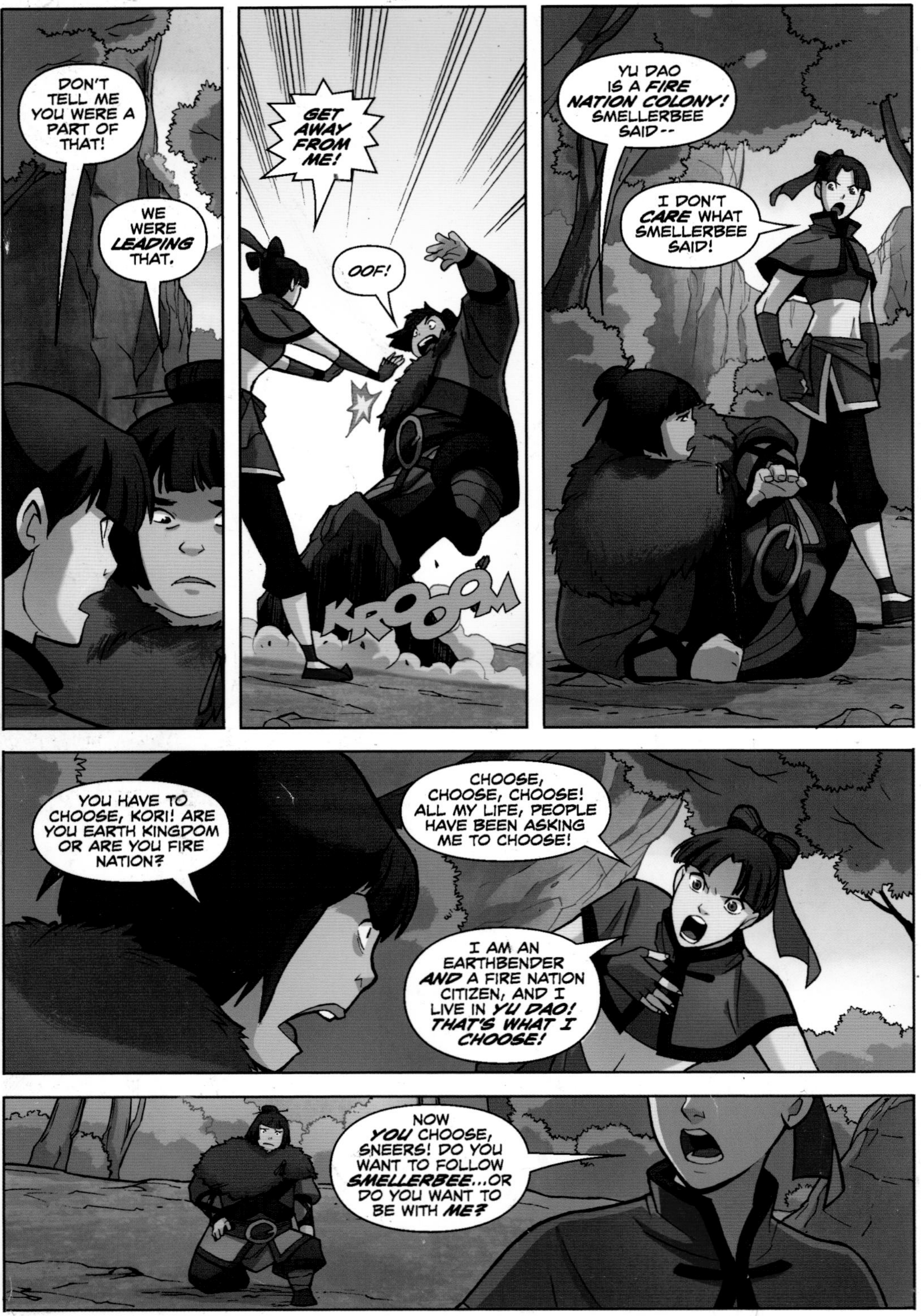
DON'T TELL ME YOU WERE A PART OF THAT!
WE WERE *LEADING* THAT.
GET AWAY FROM ME!
OOF!
KROOOOM
YU DAO IS A *FIRE NATION COLONY!* SMELLERBEE SAID--
I DON'T *CARE* WHAT SMELLERBEE SAID!
YOU HAVE TO CHOOSE, KORI! ARE YOU EARTH KINGDOM OR ARE YOU FIRE NATION?
CHOOSE, CHOOSE, CHOOSE! ALL MY LIFE, PEOPLE HAVE BEEN ASKING ME TO CHOOSE!
I AM AN EARTHBENDER *AND* A FIRE NATION CITIZEN, AND I LIVE IN *YU DAO! THAT'S WHAT I CHOOSE!*
NOW *YOU* CHOOSE, SNEERS! DO YOU WANT TO FOLLOW *SMELLERBEE*...OR DO YOU WANT TO BE WITH *ME?*

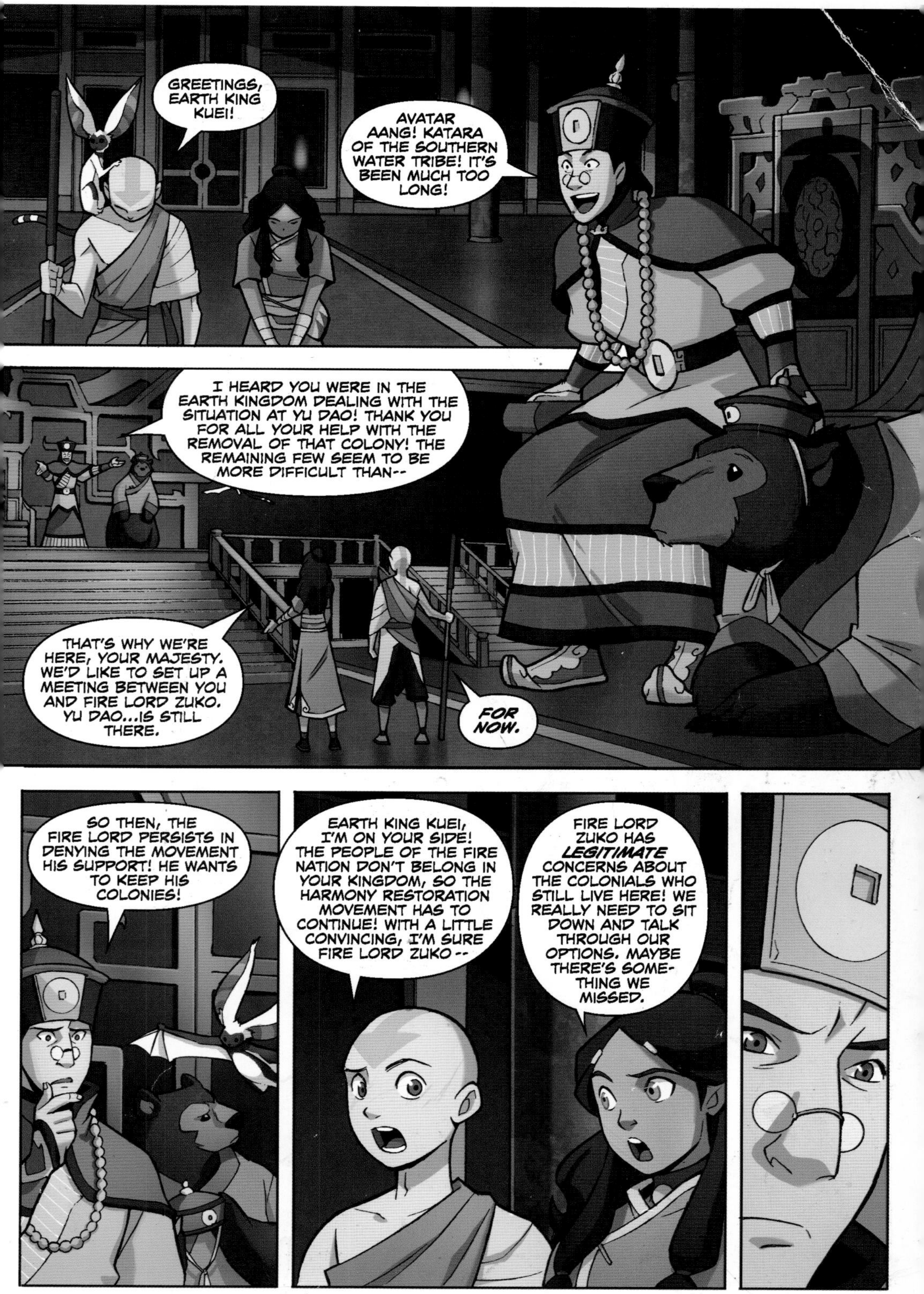
GREETINGS, EARTH KING KUEI!
AVATAR AANG! KATARA OF THE SOUTHERN WATER TRIBE! IT'S BEEN MUCH TOO LONG!
I HEARD YOU WERE IN THE EARTH KINGDOM DEALING WITH THE SITUATION AT YU DAO! THANK YOU FOR ALL YOUR HELP WITH THE REMOVAL OF THAT COLONY! THE REMAINING FEW SEEM TO BE MORE DIFFICULT THAN--
THAT'S WHY WE'RE HERE, YOUR MAJESTY. WE'D LIKE TO SET UP A MEETING BETWEEN YOU AND FIRE LORD ZUKO. YU DAO...IS STILL THERE.
FOR NOW.
SO THEN, THE FIRE LORD PERSISTS IN DENYING THE MOVEMENT HIS SUPPORT! HE WANTS TO KEEP HIS COLONIES!
EARTH KING KUEI, I'M ON YOUR SIDE! THE PEOPLE OF THE FIRE NATION DON'T BELONG IN YOUR KINGDOM, SO THE HARMONY RESTORATION MOVEMENT HAS TO CONTINUE! WITH A LITTLE CONVINCING, I'M SURE FIRE LORD ZUKO --
FIRE LORD ZUKO HAS LEGITIMATE CONCERNS ABOUT THE COLONIALS WHO STILL LIVE HERE! WE REALLY NEED TO SIT DOWN AND TALK THROUGH OUR OPTIONS. MAYBE THERE'S SOME-THING WE MISSED.

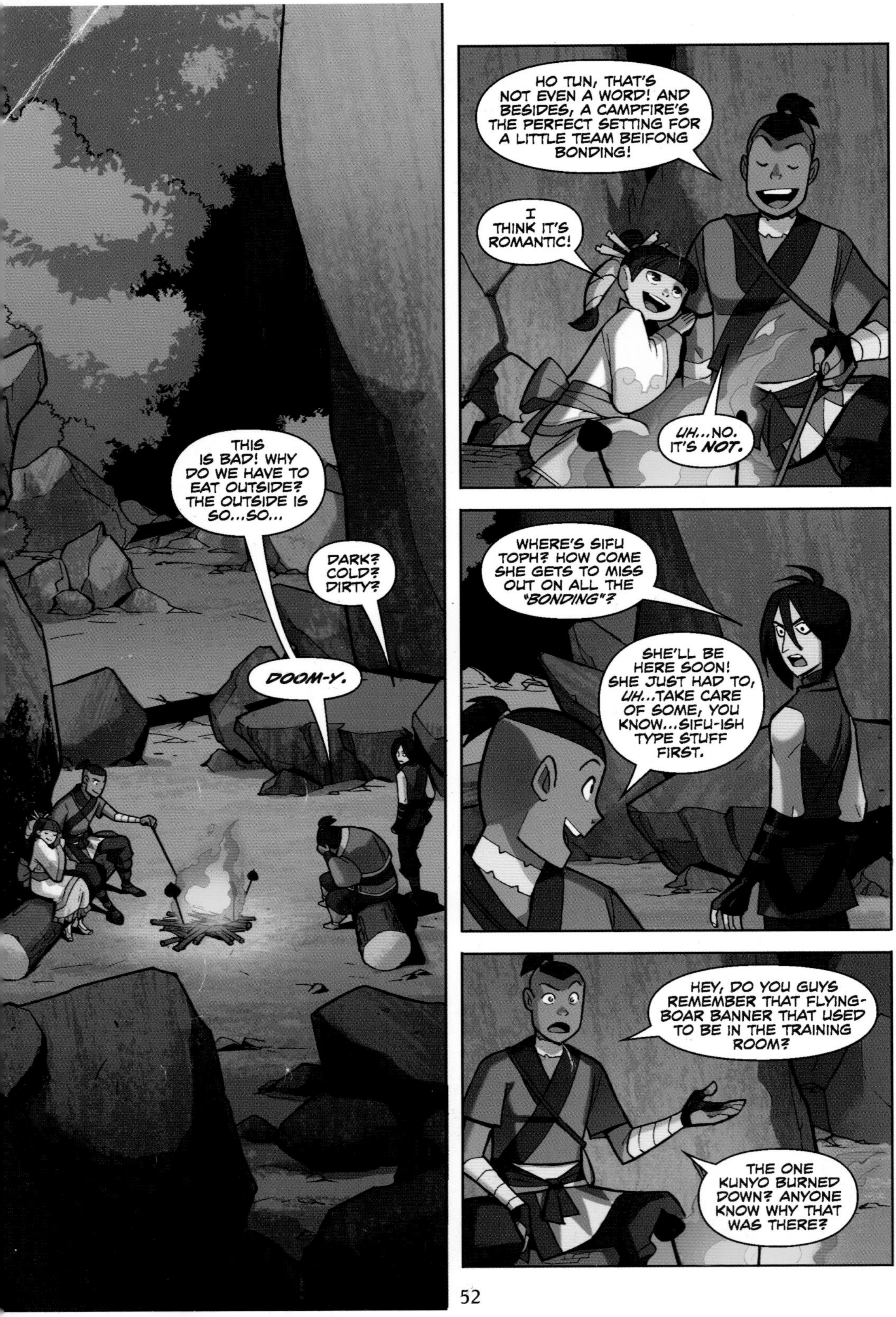
THIS IS BAD! WHY DO WE HAVE TO EAT OUTSIDE? THE OUTSIDE IS SO...SO...
DARK? COLD? DIRTY?
DOOM-Y.
HO TUN, THAT'S NOT EVEN A WORD! AND BESIDES, A CAMPFIRE'S THE PERFECT SETTING FOR A LITTLE TEAM BEIFONG BONDING!
I THINK IT'S ROMANTIC!
UH...NO. IT'S NOT.
WHERE'S SIFU TOPH? HOW COME SHE GETS TO MISS OUT ON ALL THE "BONDING"?
SHE'LL BE HERE SOON! SHE JUST HAD TO, UH...TAKE CARE OF SOME, YOU KNOW...SIFU-ISH TYPE STUFF FIRST.
HEY, DO YOU GUYS REMEMBER THAT FLYING-BOAR BANNER THAT USED TO BE IN THE TRAINING ROOM?
THE ONE KUNYO BURNED DOWN? ANYONE KNOW WHY THAT WAS THERE?

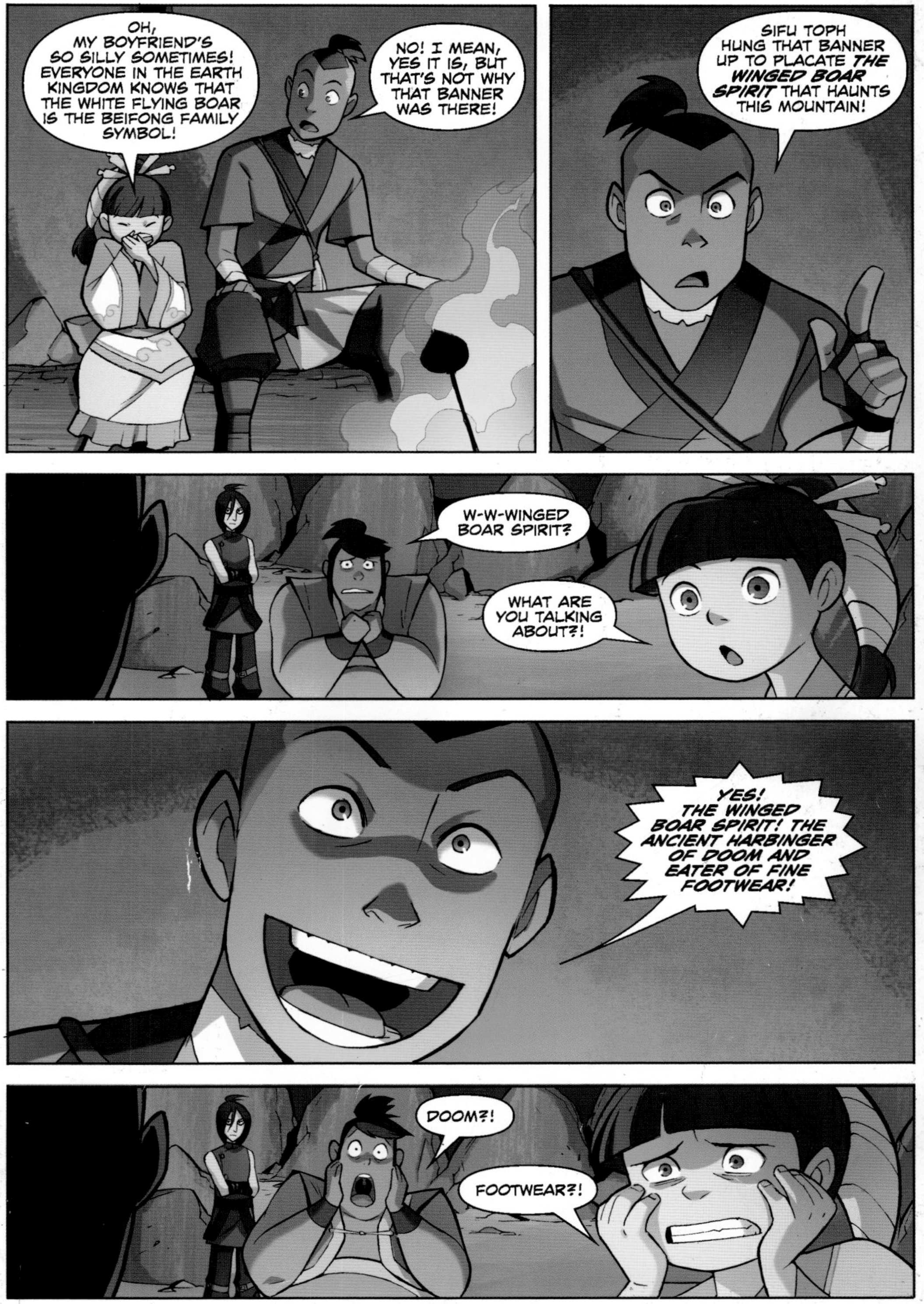
OH, MY BOYFRIEND'S SO SILLY SOMETIMES! EVERYONE IN THE EARTH KINGDOM KNOWS THAT THE WHITE FLYING BOAR IS THE BEIFONG FAMILY SYMBOL!
NO! I MEAN, YES IT IS, BUT THAT'S NOT WHY THAT BANNER WAS THERE!
SIFU TOPH HUNG THAT BANNER UP TO PLACATE THE WINGED BOAR SPIRIT THAT HAUNTS THIS MOUNTAIN!
W-W-WINGED BOAR SPIRIT?
WHAT ARE YOU TALKING ABOUT?!
YES! THE WINGED BOAR SPIRIT! THE ANCIENT HARBINGER OF DOOM AND EATER OF FINE FOOTWEAR!
DOOM?!
FOOTWEAR?!

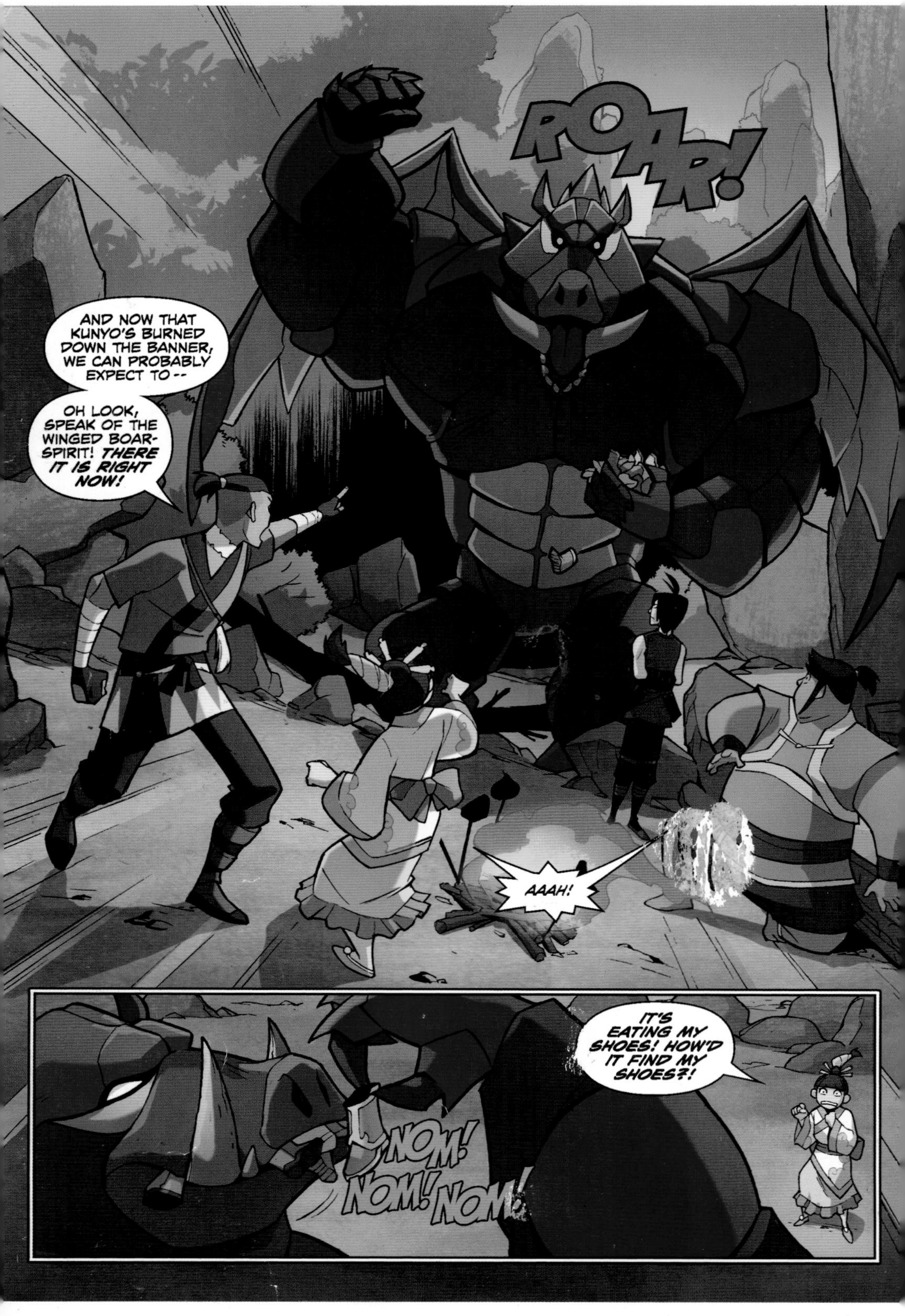
ROAR!
AND NOW THAT KUNYO'S BURNED DOWN THE BANNER, WE CAN PROBABLY EXPECT TO --
OH LOOK, SPEAK OF THE WINGED BOAR-SPIRIT! *THERE IT IS RIGHT NOW!*
AAAH!
IT'S EATING MY SHOES! HOW'D IT FIND MY SHOES?!
NOM! NOM! NOM!

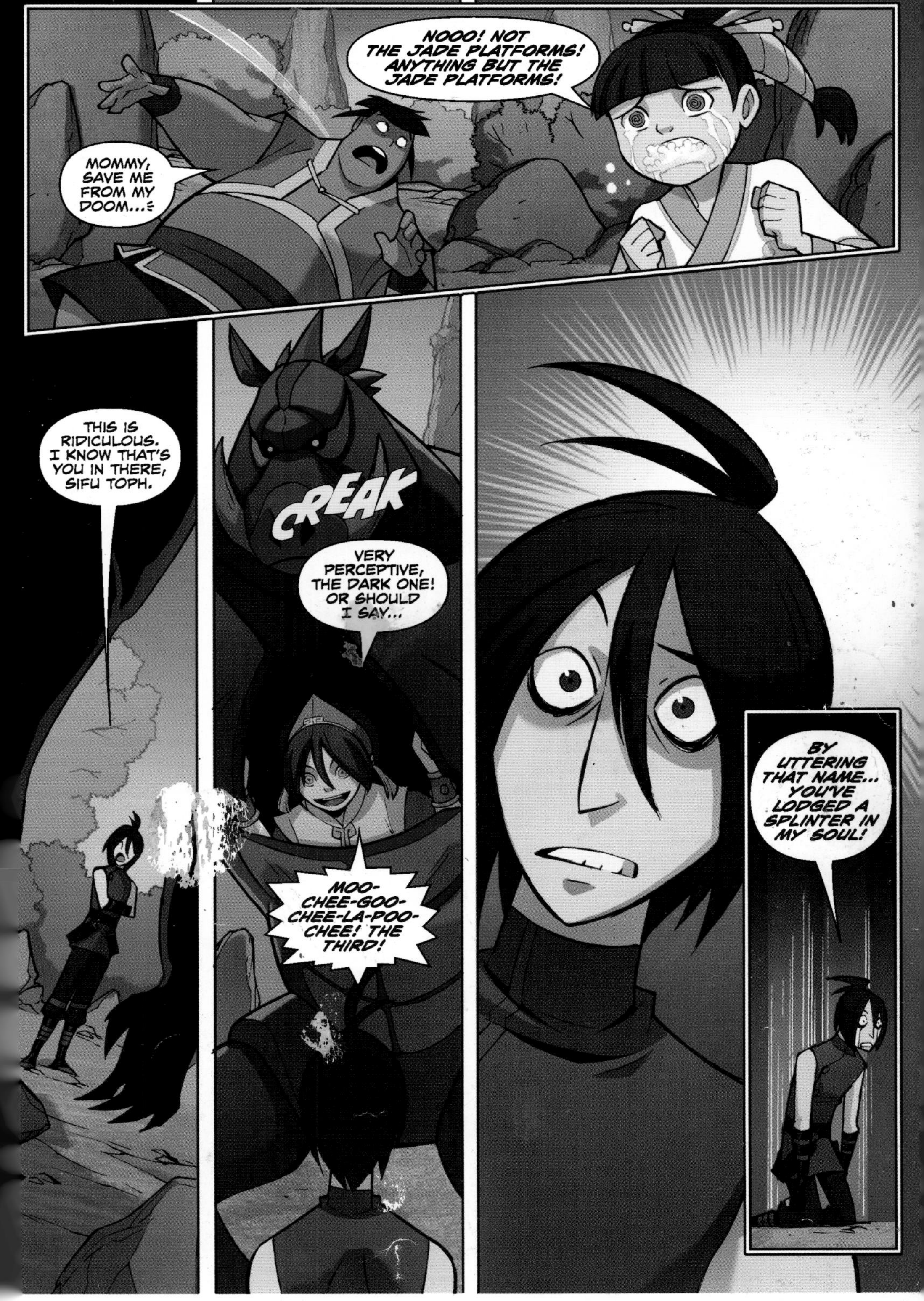
NOOO! NOT THE JADE PLATFORMS! ANYTHING BUT THE JADE PLATFORMS!
MOMMY, SAVE ME FROM MY DOOM...
THIS IS RIDICULOUS. I KNOW THAT'S YOU IN THERE, SIFU TOPH.
CREAK
VERY PERCEPTIVE, THE DARK ONE! OR SHOULD I SAY...
MOO-CHEE-GOO-CHEE-LA-POO-CHEE! THE THIRD!
BY UTTERING THAT NAME... YOU'VE LODGED A SPLINTER IN MY SOUL!

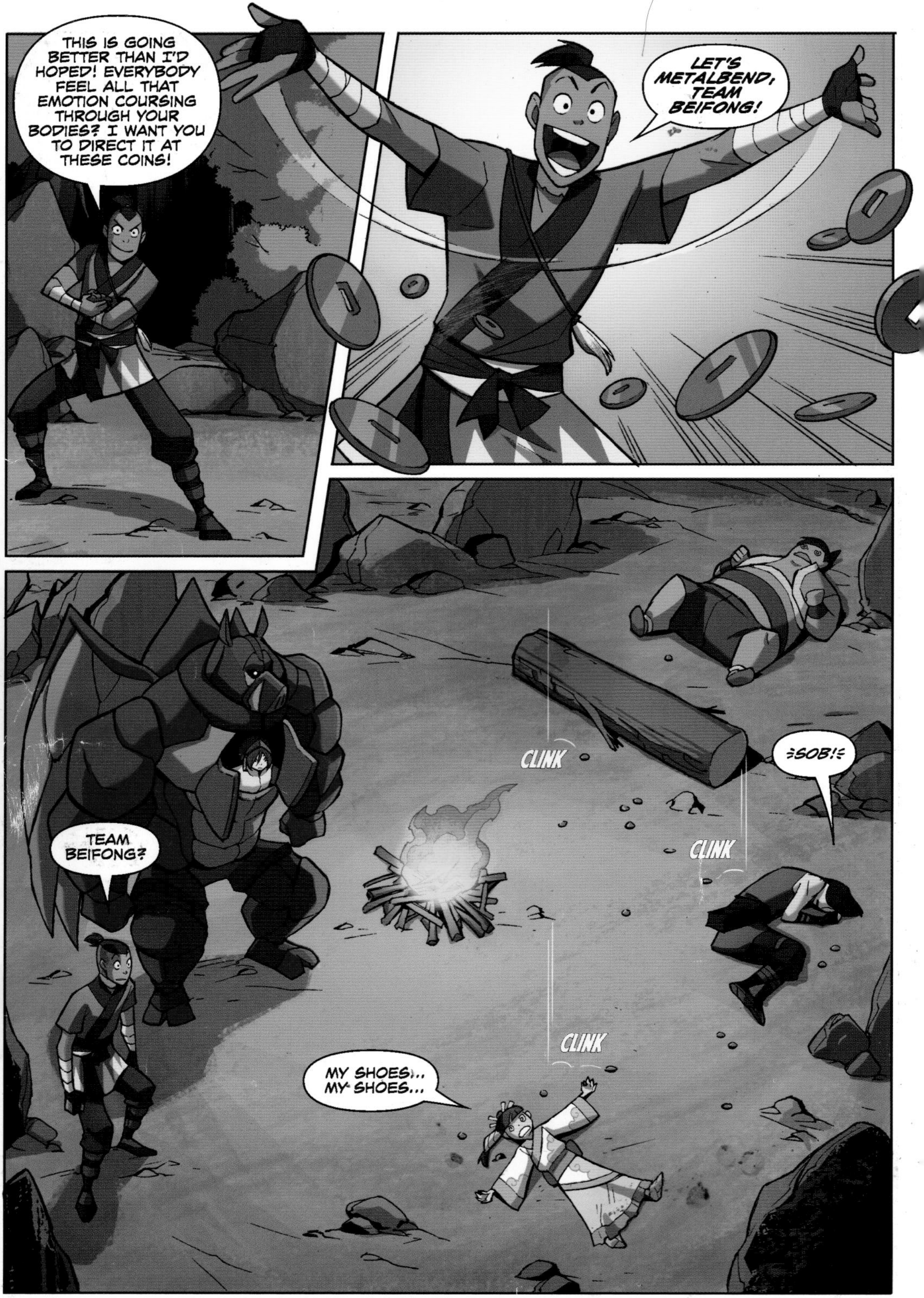
THIS IS GOING BETTER THAN I'D HOPED! EVERYBODY FEEL ALL THAT EMOTION COURSING THROUGH YOUR BODIES? I WANT YOU TO DIRECT IT AT THESE COINS!
LET'S METALBEND, TEAM BEIFONG!
TEAM BEIFONG?
CLINK
SOB!
CLINK
CLINK
MY SHOES... MY SHOES...

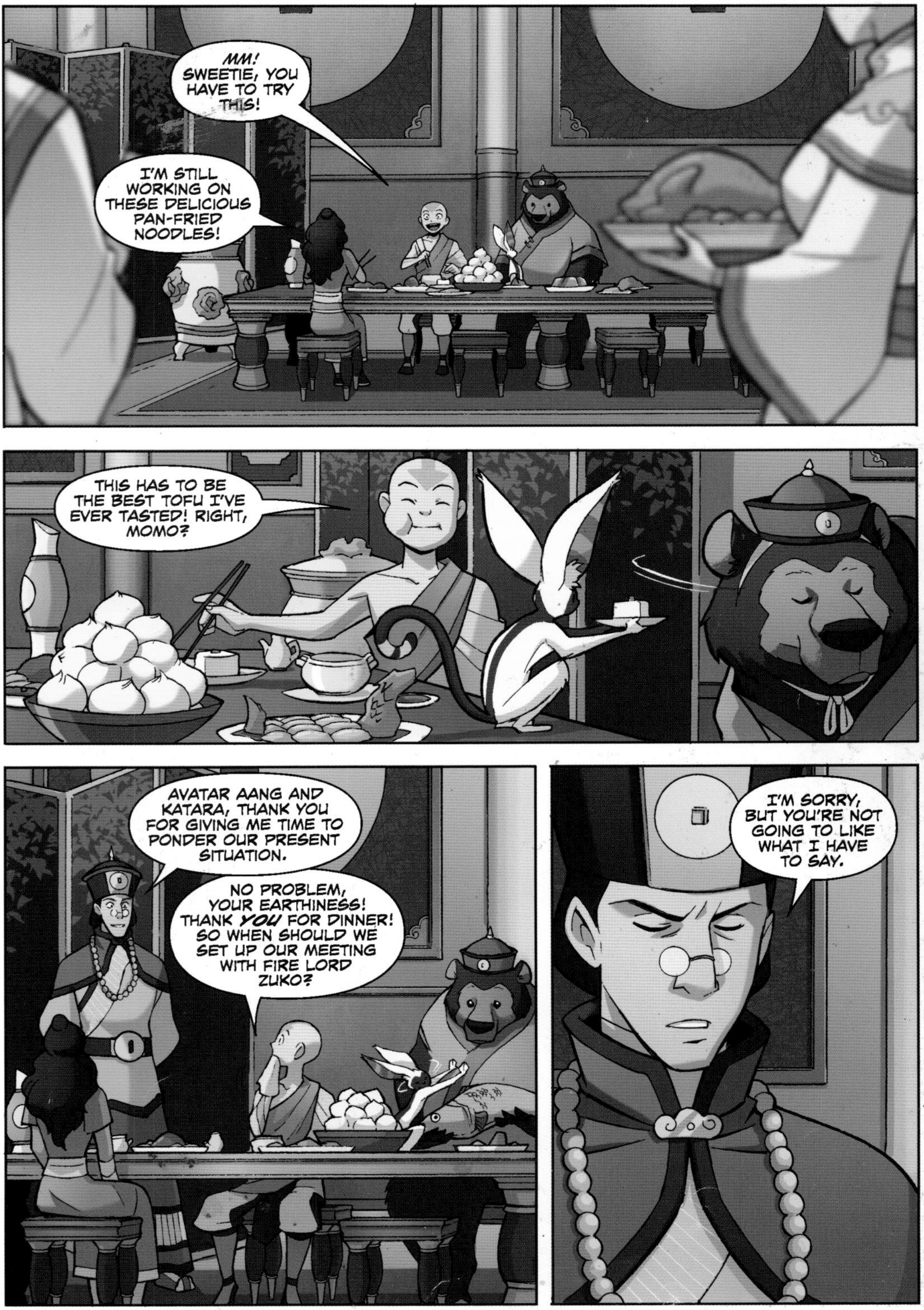
MM! SWEETIE, YOU HAVE TO TRY THIS!
I'M STILL WORKING ON THESE DELICIOUS PAN-FRIED NOODLES!
THIS HAS TO BE THE BEST TOFU I'VE EVER TASTED! RIGHT, MOMO?
AVATAR AANG AND KATARA, THANK YOU FOR GIVING ME TIME TO PONDER OUR PRESENT SITUATION.
NO PROBLEM, YOUR EARTHINESS! THANK YOU FOR DINNER! SO WHEN SHOULD WE SET UP OUR MEETING WITH FIRE LORD ZUKO?
I'M SORRY, BUT YOU'RE NOT GOING TO LIKE WHAT I HAVE TO SAY.

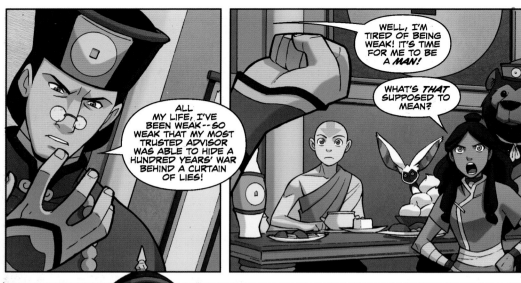

ALL MY LIFE, I'VE BEEN WEAK--SO WEAK THAT MY MOST TRUSTED ADVISOR WAS ABLE TO HIDE A HUNDRED YEARS' WAR BEHIND A CURTAIN OF LIES!

WELL, I'M TIRED OF BEING WEAK! IT'S TIME FOR ME TO BE A *MAN!*

WHAT'S *THAT* SUPPOSED TO MEAN?

FIRE LORD ZUKO PROMISED HE WOULD SEE THE HARMONY RESTORATION MOVEMENT THROUGH TO THE VERY END. NOW HE'S TURNED HIS PROMISE INTO A LIE! WHY SHOULD I MEET WITH HIM-- SO HE CAN TELL ME MORE LIES?

I WILL NOT STAND FOR ANY MORE LIES!

I WILL ORDER GENERAL HOW TO LEAD MY TROOPS TO YU DAO AND *ENFORCE HARMONY!*

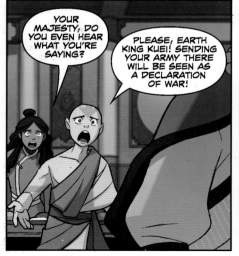

YOUR MAJESTY, DO YOU EVEN HEAR WHAT YOU'RE SAYING?

PLEASE, EARTH KING KUEI! SENDING YOUR ARMY THERE WILL BE SEEN AS A DECLARATION OF WAR!

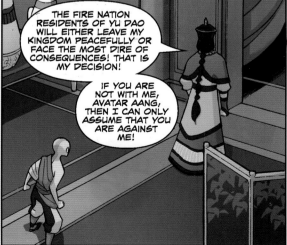

THE FIRE NATION RESIDENTS OF YU DAO WILL EITHER LEAVE MY KINGDOM PEACEFULLY OR FACE THE MOST DIRE OF CONSEQUENCES! THAT IS MY DECISION!

IF YOU ARE NOT WITH ME, AVATAR AANG, THEN I CAN ONLY ASSUME THAT YOU ARE AGAINST ME!

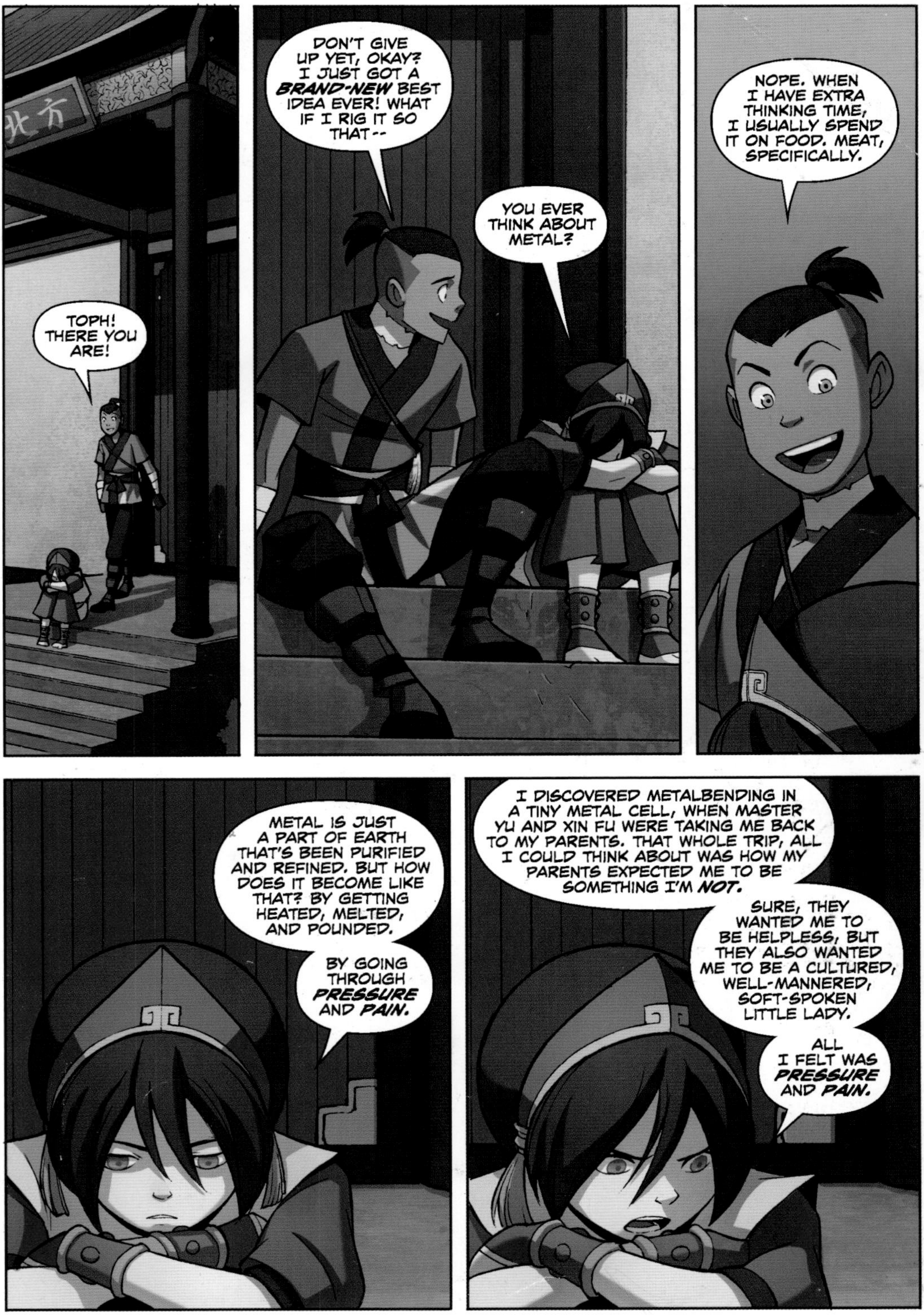
北方
TOPH! THERE YOU ARE!
DON'T GIVE UP YET, OKAY? I JUST GOT A BRAND-NEW BEST IDEA EVER! WHAT IF I RIG IT SO THAT--
YOU EVER THINK ABOUT METAL?
NOPE. WHEN I HAVE EXTRA THINKING TIME, I USUALLY SPEND IT ON FOOD. MEAT, SPECIFICALLY.
METAL IS JUST A PART OF EARTH THAT'S BEEN PURIFIED AND REFINED. BUT HOW DOES IT BECOME LIKE THAT? BY GETTING HEATED, MELTED, AND POUNDED.
BY GOING THROUGH PRESSURE AND PAIN.
I DISCOVERED METALBENDING IN A TINY METAL CELL, WHEN MASTER YU AND XIN FU WERE TAKING ME BACK TO MY PARENTS. THAT WHOLE TRIP, ALL I COULD THINK ABOUT WAS HOW MY PARENTS EXPECTED ME TO BE SOMETHING I'M NOT.
SURE, THEY WANTED ME TO BE HELPLESS, BUT THEY ALSO WANTED ME TO BE A CULTURED, WELL-MANNERED, SOFT-SPOKEN LITTLE LADY.
ALL I FELT WAS PRESSURE AND PAIN.

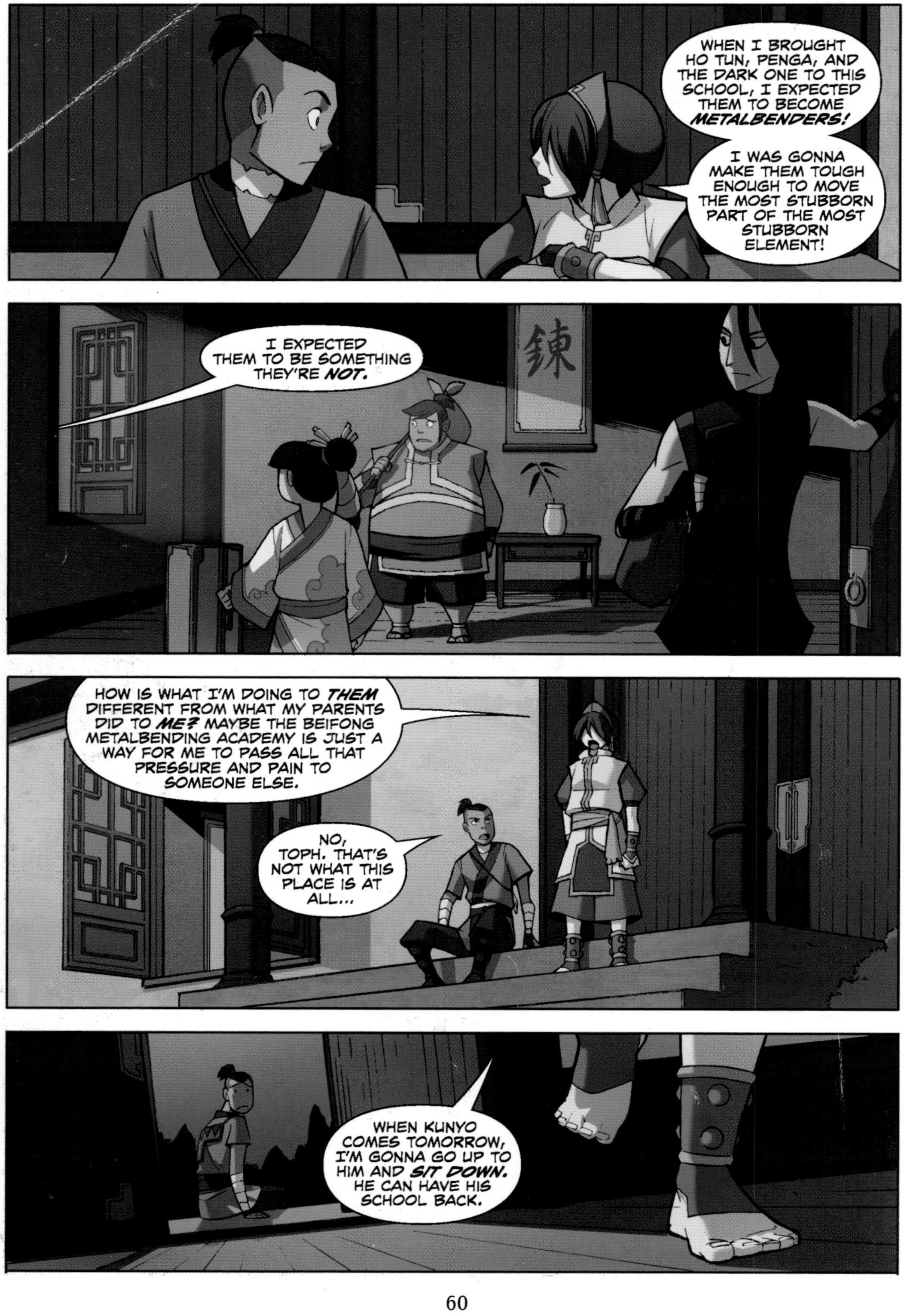
WHEN I BROUGHT HO TUN, PENGA, AND THE DARK ONE TO THIS SCHOOL, I EXPECTED THEM TO BECOME *METALBENDERS!*
I WAS GONNA MAKE THEM TOUGH ENOUGH TO MOVE THE MOST STUBBORN PART OF THE MOST STUBBORN ELEMENT!
I EXPECTED THEM TO BE SOMETHING THEY'RE *NOT.*
HOW IS WHAT I'M DOING TO *THEM* DIFFERENT FROM WHAT MY PARENTS DID TO *ME?* MAYBE THE BEIFONG METALBENDING ACADEMY IS JUST A WAY FOR ME TO PASS ALL THAT PRESSURE AND PAIN TO SOMEONE ELSE.
NO, TOPH. THAT'S NOT WHAT THIS PLACE IS AT ALL...
WHEN KUNYO COMES TOMORROW, I'M GONNA GO UP TO HIM AND *SIT DOWN.* HE CAN HAVE HIS SCHOOL BACK.

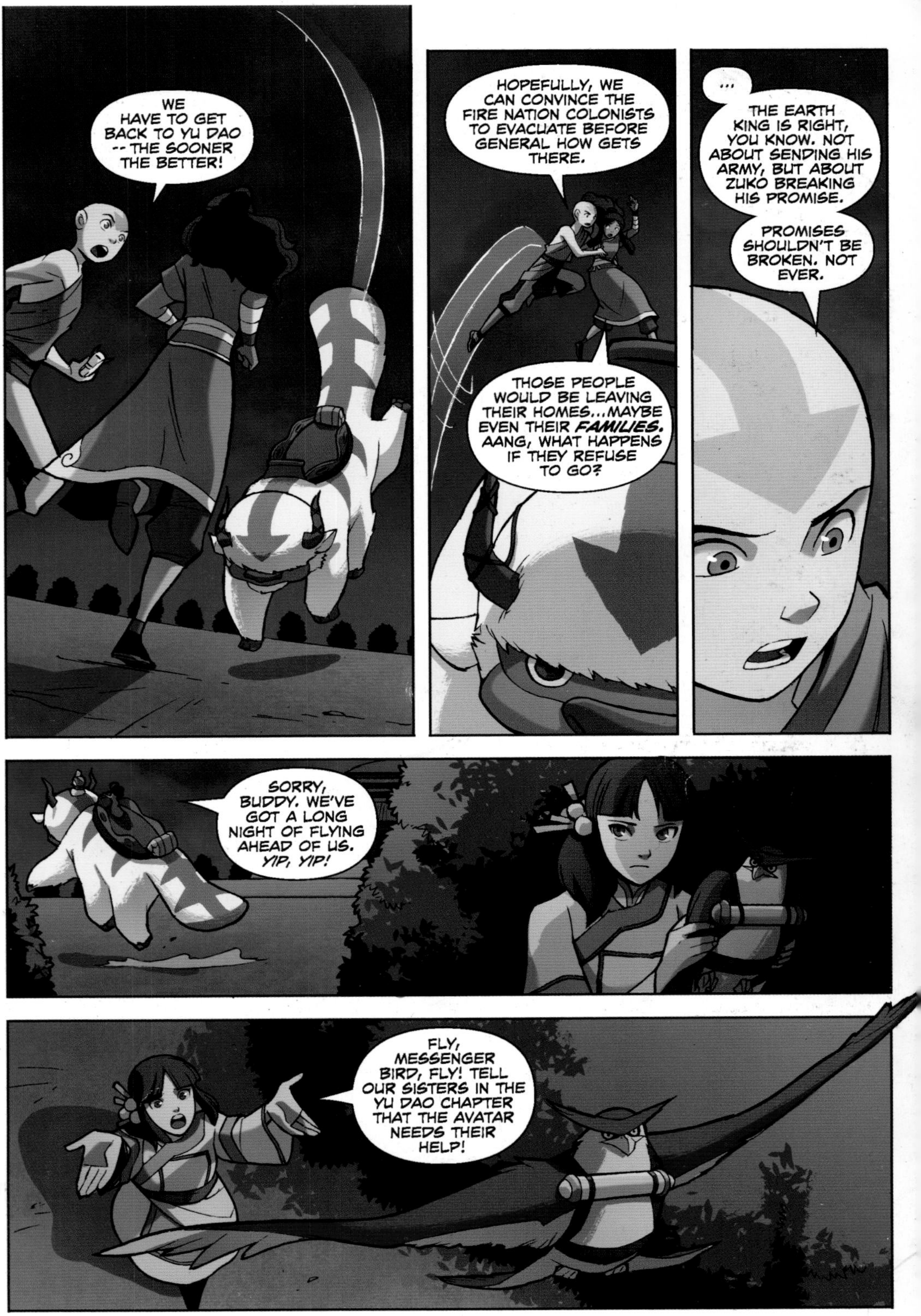
WE HAVE TO GET BACK TO YU DAO -- THE SOONER THE BETTER!
HOPEFULLY, WE CAN CONVINCE THE FIRE NATION COLONISTS TO EVACUATE BEFORE GENERAL HOW GETS THERE.
THOSE PEOPLE WOULD BE LEAVING THEIR HOMES...MAYBE EVEN THEIR *FAMILIES.* AANG, WHAT HAPPENS IF THEY REFUSE TO GO?
...
THE EARTH KING IS RIGHT, YOU KNOW. NOT ABOUT SENDING HIS ARMY, BUT ABOUT ZUKO BREAKING HIS PROMISE.
PROMISES SHOULDN'T BE BROKEN. NOT EVER.
SORRY, BUDDY. WE'VE GOT A LONG NIGHT OF FLYING AHEAD OF US. *YIP, YIP!*
FLY, MESSENGER BIRD, FLY! TELL OUR SISTERS IN THE YU DAO CHAPTER THAT THE AVATAR NEEDS THEIR HELP!

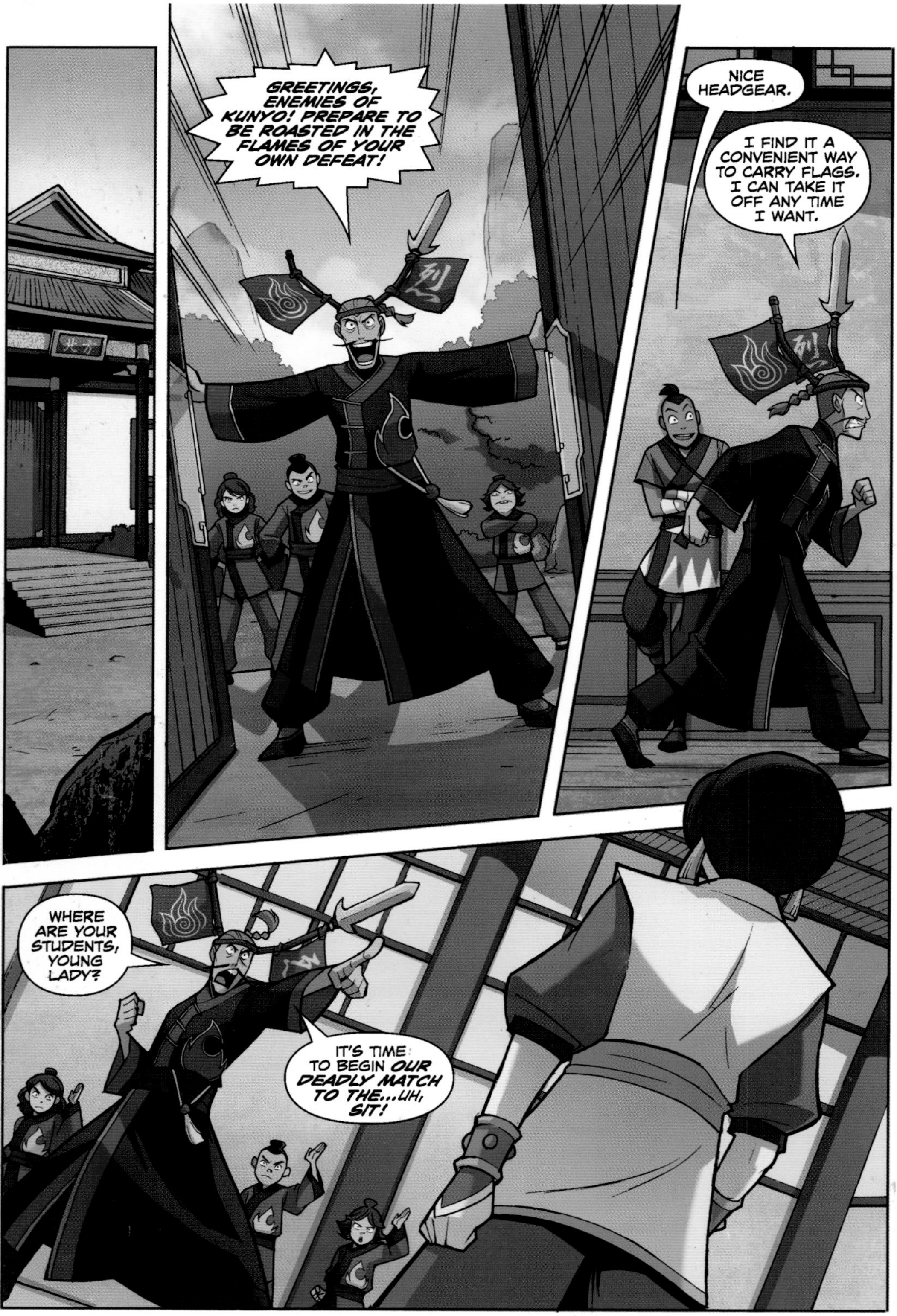
GREETINGS, ENEMIES OF KUNYO! PREPARE TO BE ROASTED IN THE FLAMES OF YOUR OWN DEFEAT!
NICE HEADGEAR.
I FIND IT A CONVENIENT WAY TO CARRY FLAGS. I CAN TAKE IT OFF ANY TIME I WANT.
WHERE ARE YOUR STUDENTS, YOUNG LADY?
IT'S TIME TO BEGIN OUR DEADLY MATCH TO THE...UH, SIT!

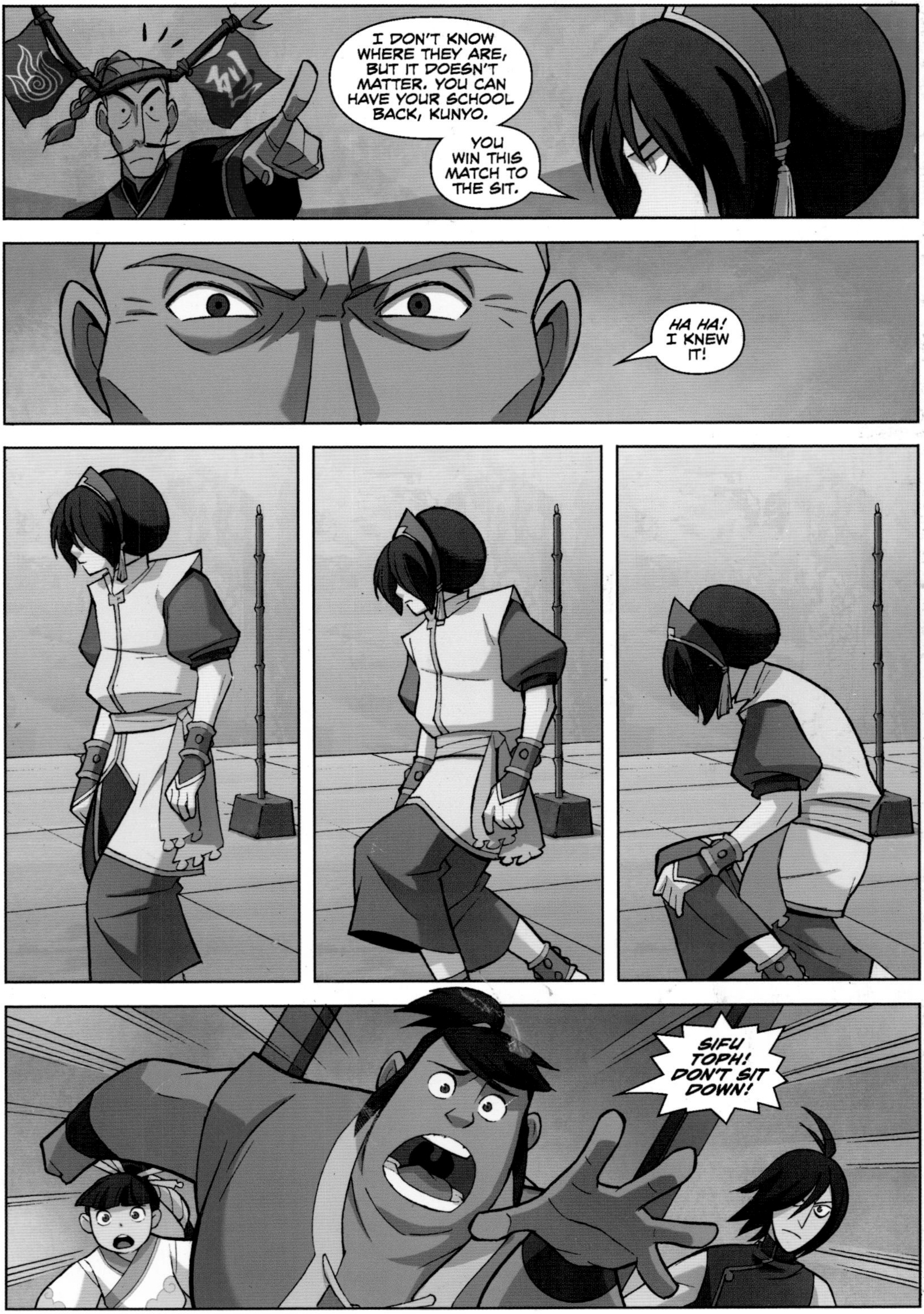
I DON'T KNOW WHERE THEY ARE, BUT IT DOESN'T MATTER. YOU CAN HAVE YOUR SCHOOL BACK, KUNYO.
YOU WIN THIS MATCH TO THE SIT.
HA HA! I KNEW IT!
SIFU TOPH! DON'T SIT DOWN!

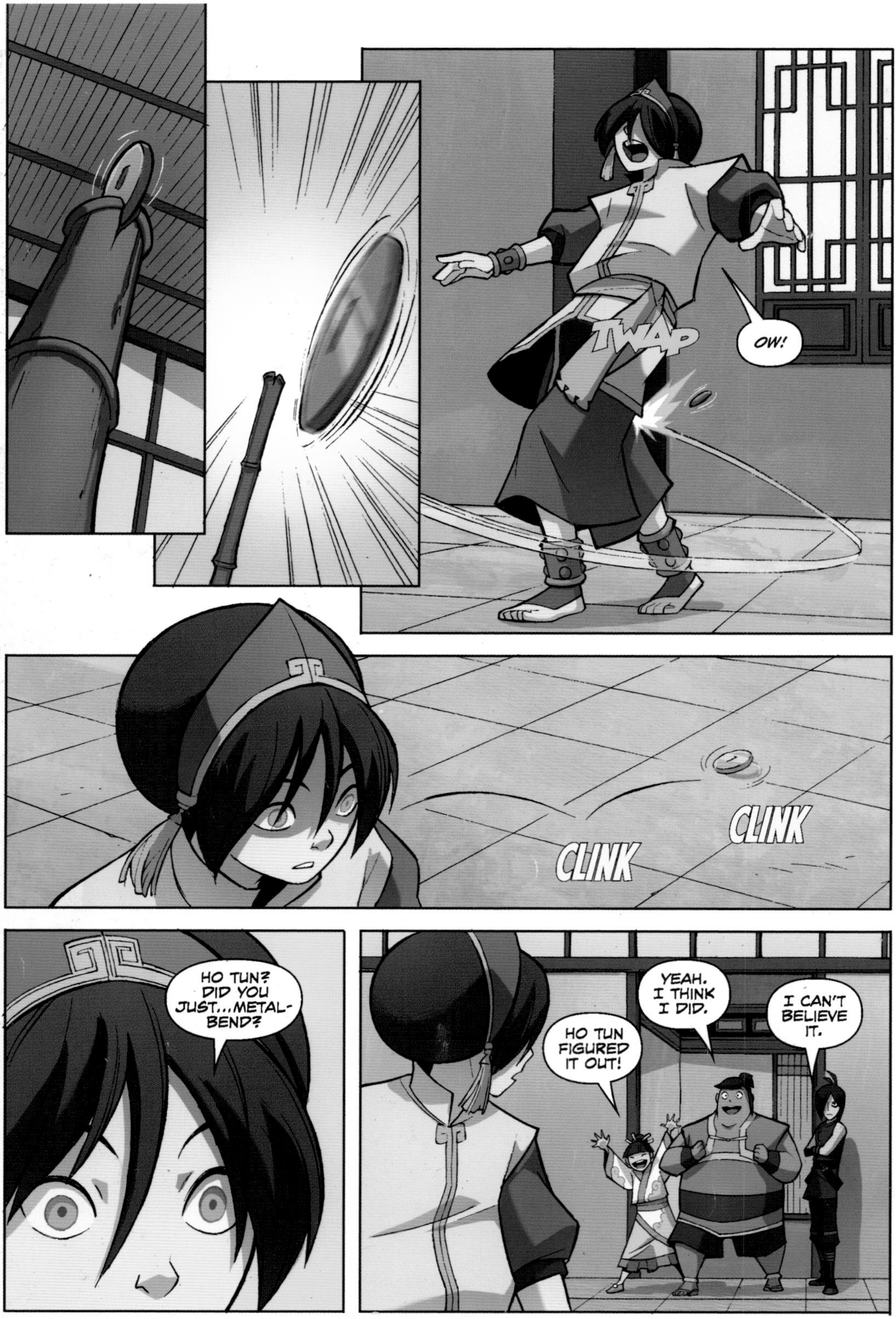
TWAP
OW!
CLINK
CLINK
HO TUN? DID YOU JUST...METAL-BEND?
HO TUN FIGURED IT OUT!
YEAH. I THINK I DID.
I CAN'T BELIEVE IT.

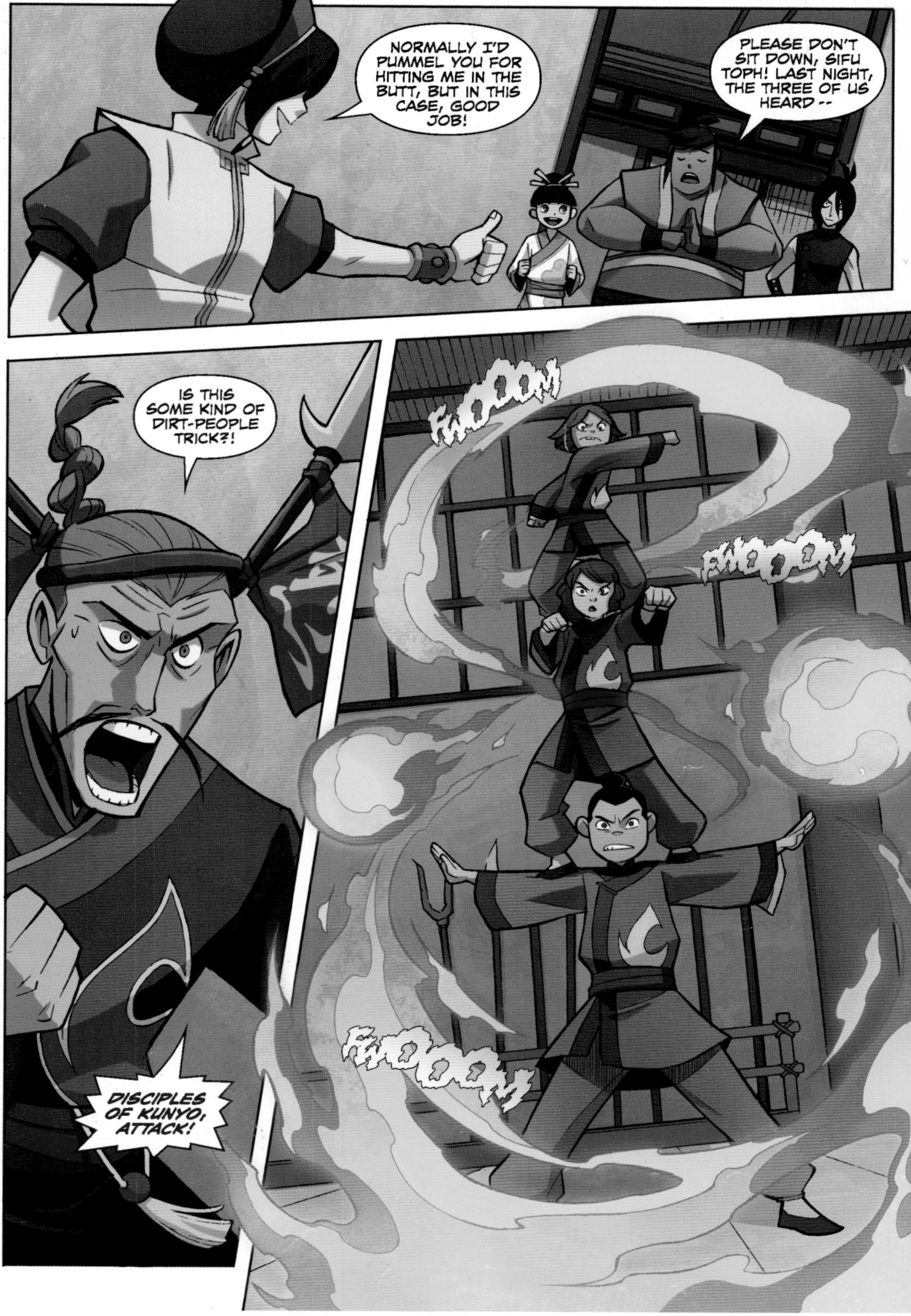
NORMALLY I'D PUMMEL YOU FOR HITTING ME IN THE BUTT, BUT IN THIS CASE, GOOD JOB!
PLEASE DON'T SIT DOWN, SIFU TOPH! LAST NIGHT, THE THREE OF US HEARD --
IS THIS SOME KIND OF DIRT-PEOPLE TRICK?!
DISCIPLES OF KUNYO, ATTACK!
FWOOOM
FWOOOM
FWOOOM

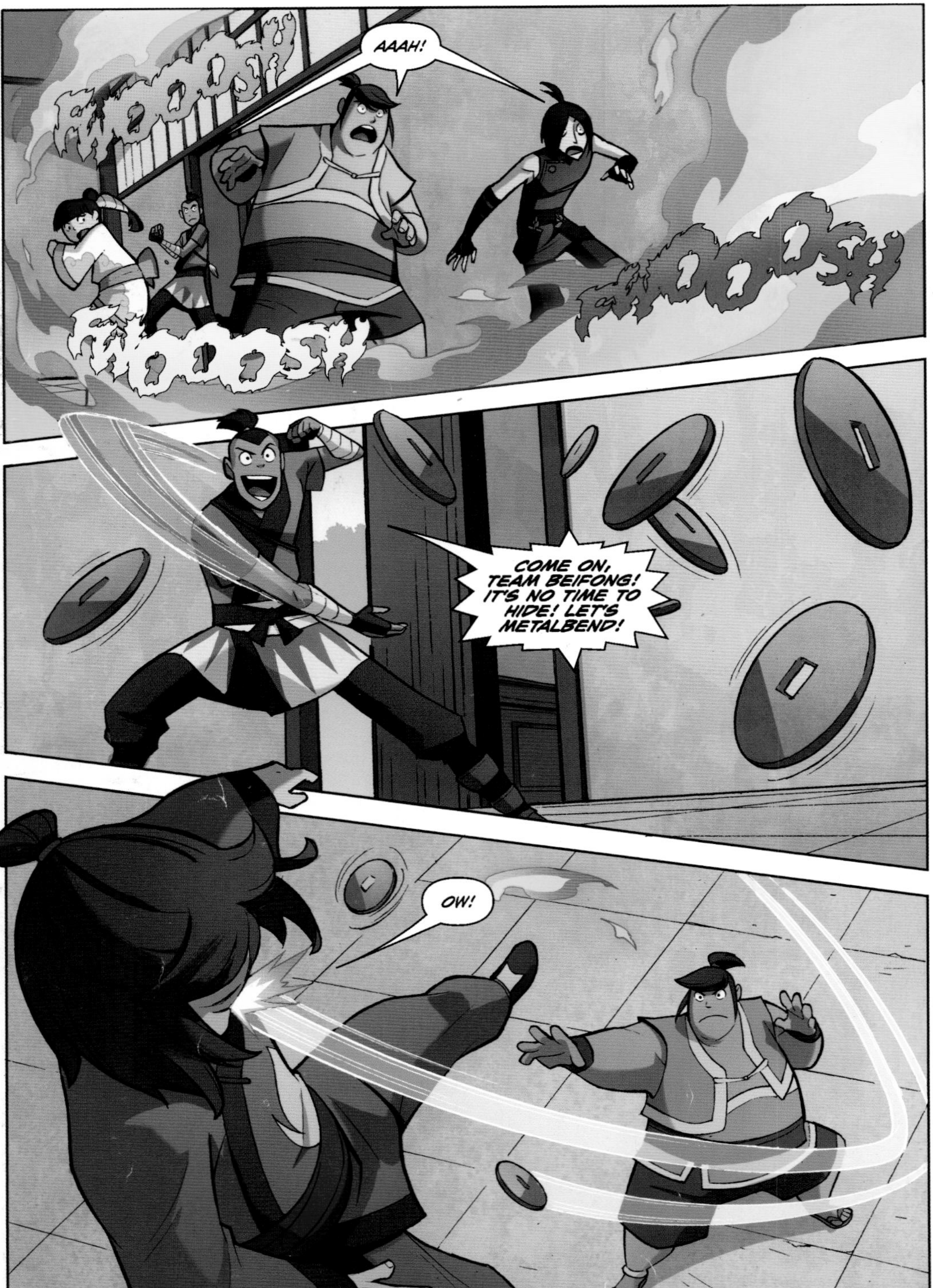
FWOOOSH
AAAH!
FWOOOSH
FWOOOSH
COME ON, TEAM BEIFONG! IT'S NO TIME TO HIDE! LET'S METALBEND!
OW!

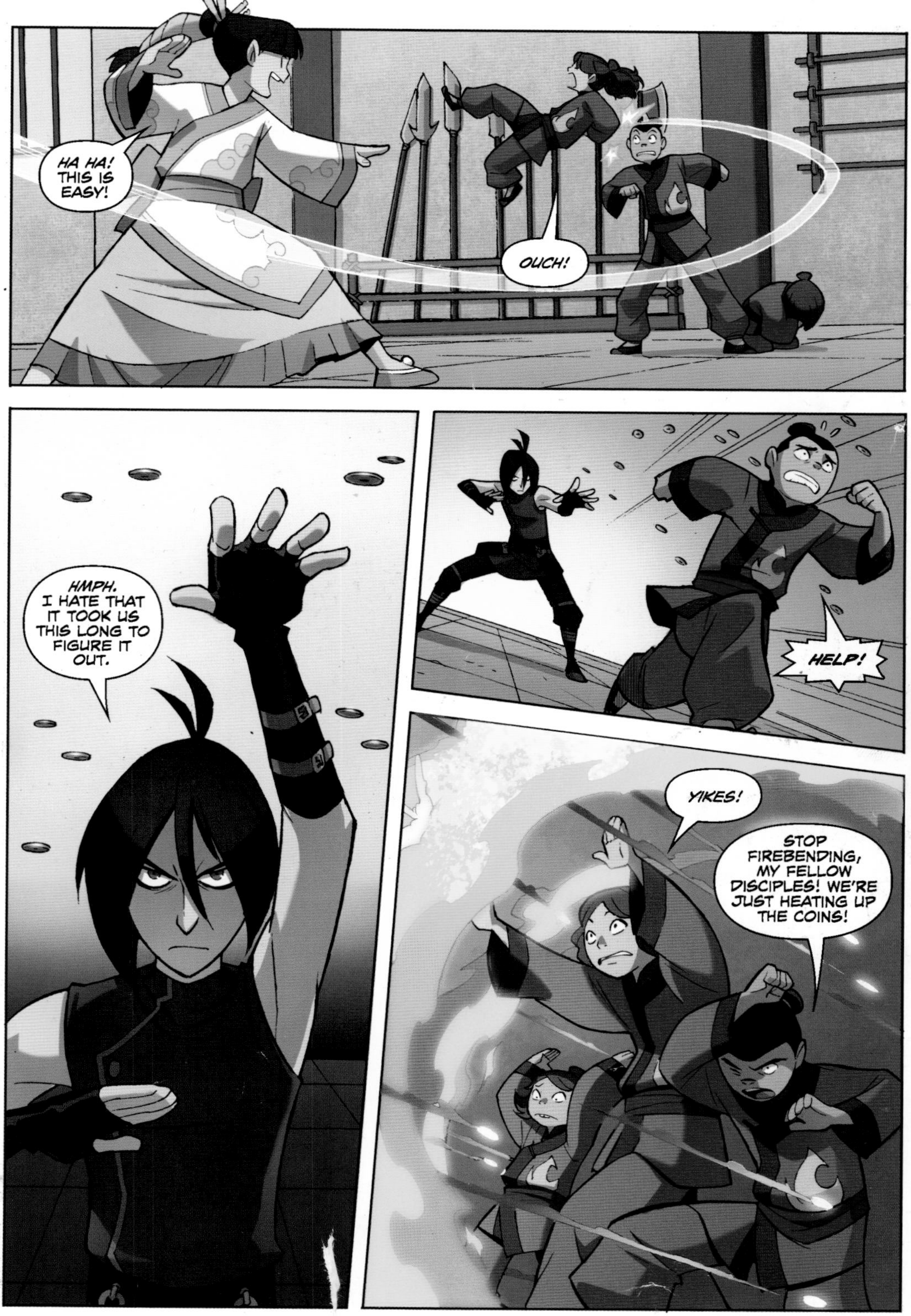
HA HA! THIS IS EASY!
OUCH!
HMPH. I HATE THAT IT TOOK US THIS LONG TO FIGURE IT OUT.
HELP!
YIKES!
STOP FIREBENDING, MY FELLOW DISCIPLES! WE'RE JUST HEATING UP THE COINS!

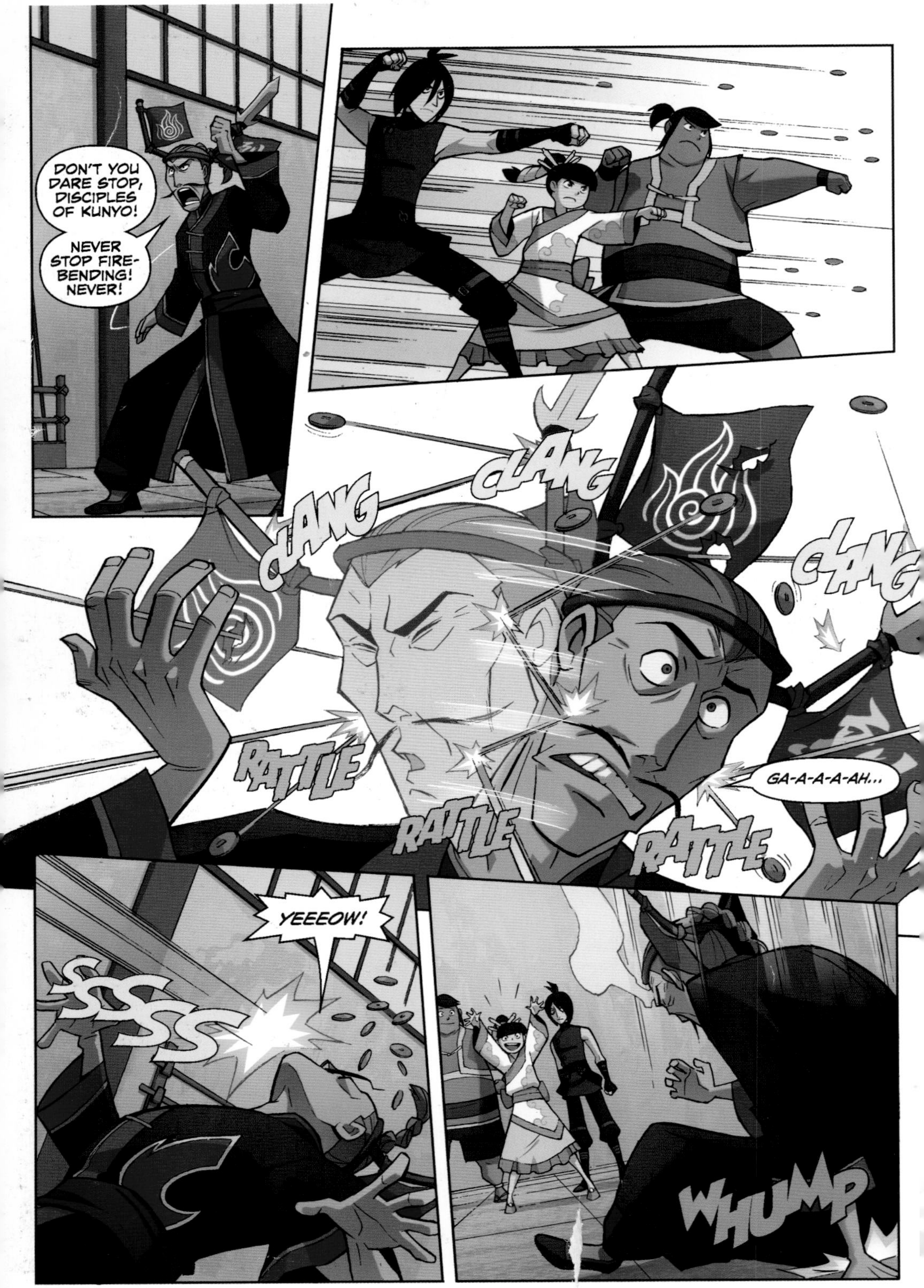
DON'T YOU DARE STOP, DISCIPLES OF KUNYO!
NEVER STOP FIRE-BENDING! NEVER!
CLANG
CLANG
CLANG
RATTLE
RATTLE
RATTLE
GA-A-A-A-AH...
YEEEOW!
SSSSS
WHUMP

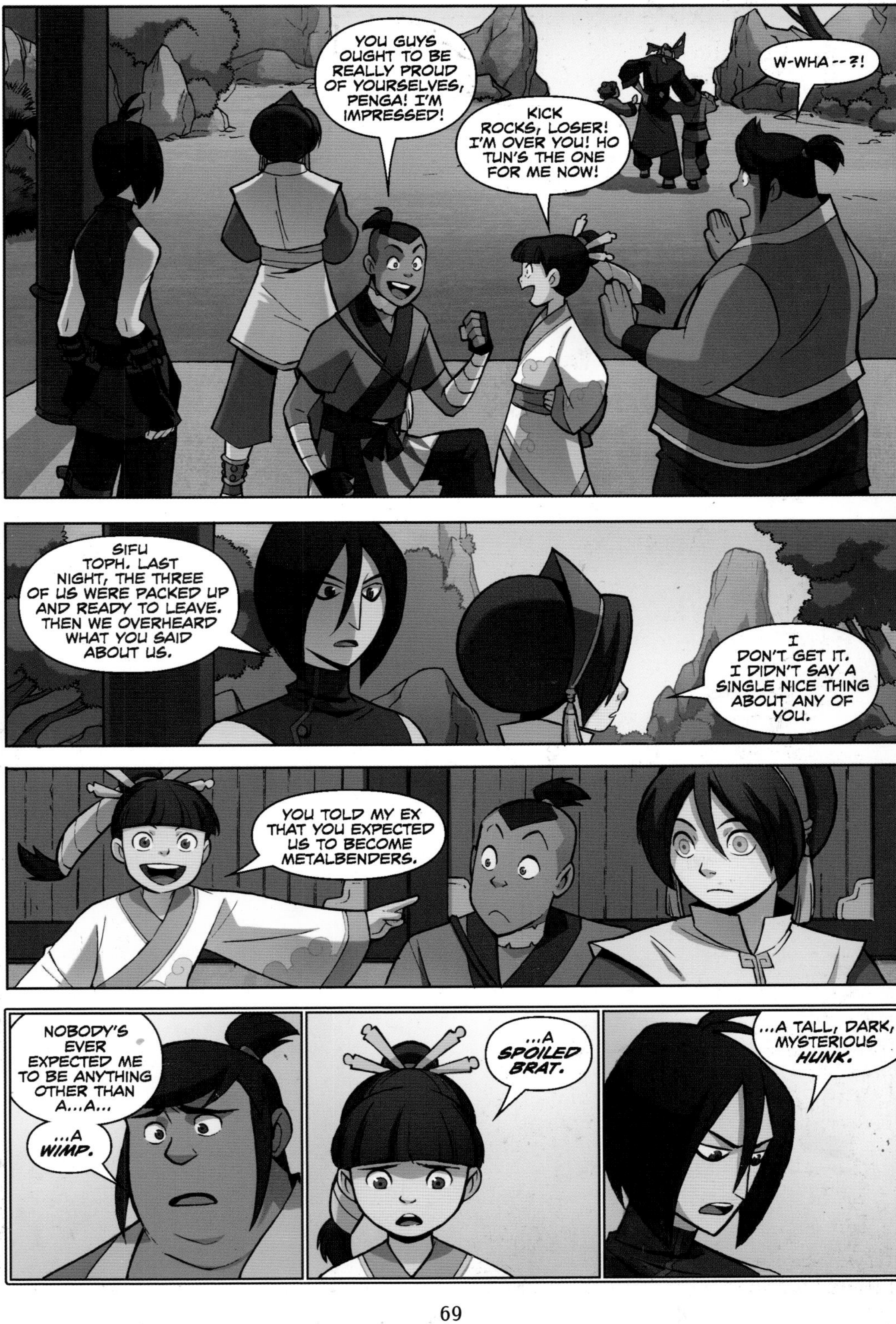
YOU GUYS OUGHT TO BE REALLY PROUD OF YOURSELVES, PENGA! I'M IMPRESSED!
KICK ROCKS, LOSER! I'M OVER YOU! HO TUN'S THE ONE FOR ME NOW!
W-WHA--?!
SIFU TOPH. LAST NIGHT, THE THREE OF US WERE PACKED UP AND READY TO LEAVE. THEN WE OVERHEARD WHAT YOU SAID ABOUT US.
I DON'T GET IT. I DIDN'T SAY A SINGLE NICE THING ABOUT ANY OF YOU.
YOU TOLD MY EX THAT YOU EXPECTED US TO BECOME METALBENDERS.
NOBODY'S EVER EXPECTED ME TO BE ANYTHING OTHER THAN A...A...
...A *WIMP.*
...A *SPOILED BRAT.*
...A TALL, DARK, MYSTERIOUS *HUNK.*

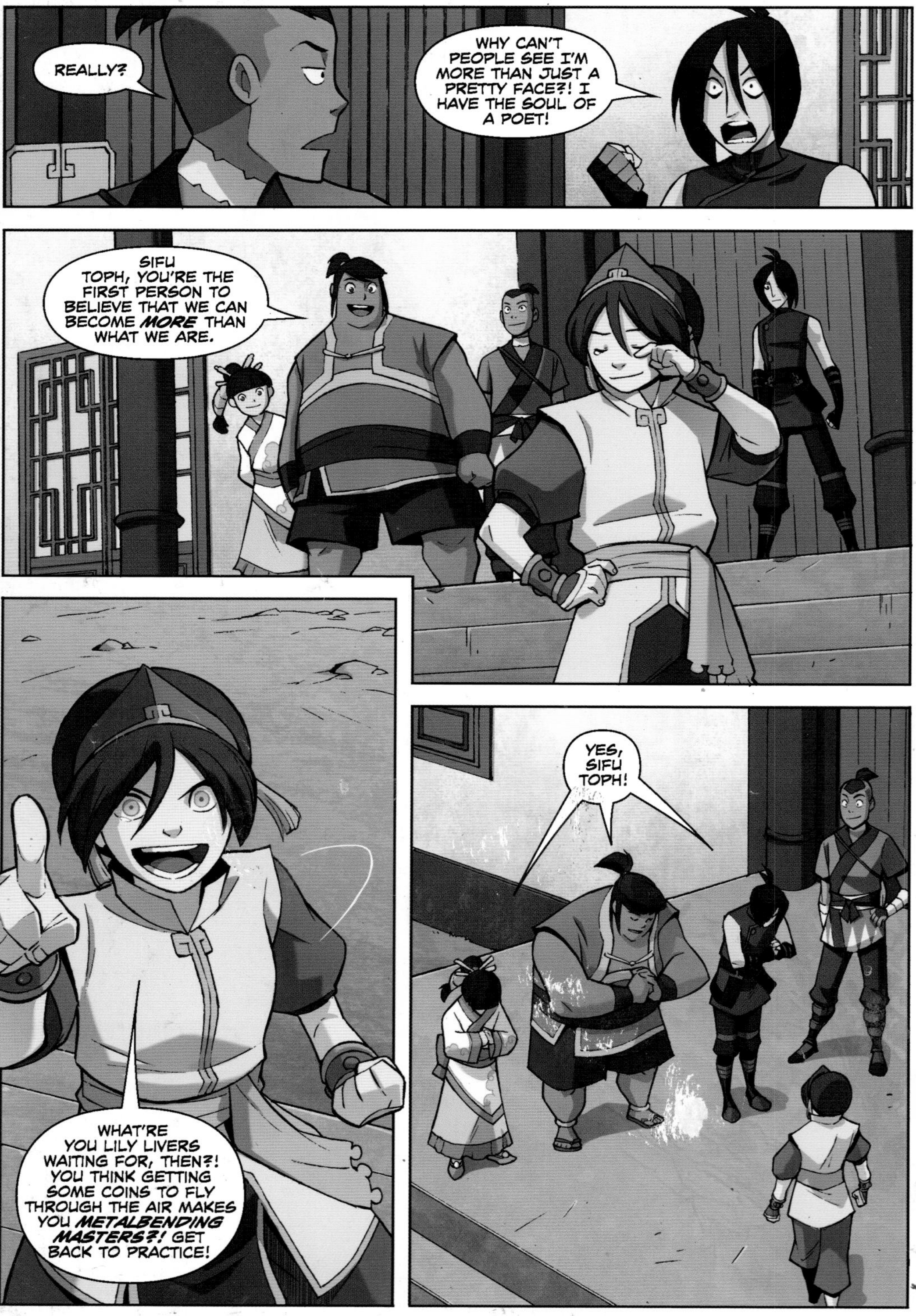
REALLY?
WHY CAN'T PEOPLE SEE I'M MORE THAN JUST A PRETTY FACE?! I HAVE THE SOUL OF A POET!
SIFU TOPH, YOU'RE THE FIRST PERSON TO BELIEVE THAT WE CAN BECOME *MORE* THAN WHAT WE ARE.
WHAT'RE YOU LILY LIVERS WAITING FOR, THEN?! YOU THINK GETTING SOME COINS TO FLY THROUGH THE AIR MAKES YOU *METALBENDING MASTERS?!* GET BACK TO PRACTICE!
YES, SIFU TOPH!

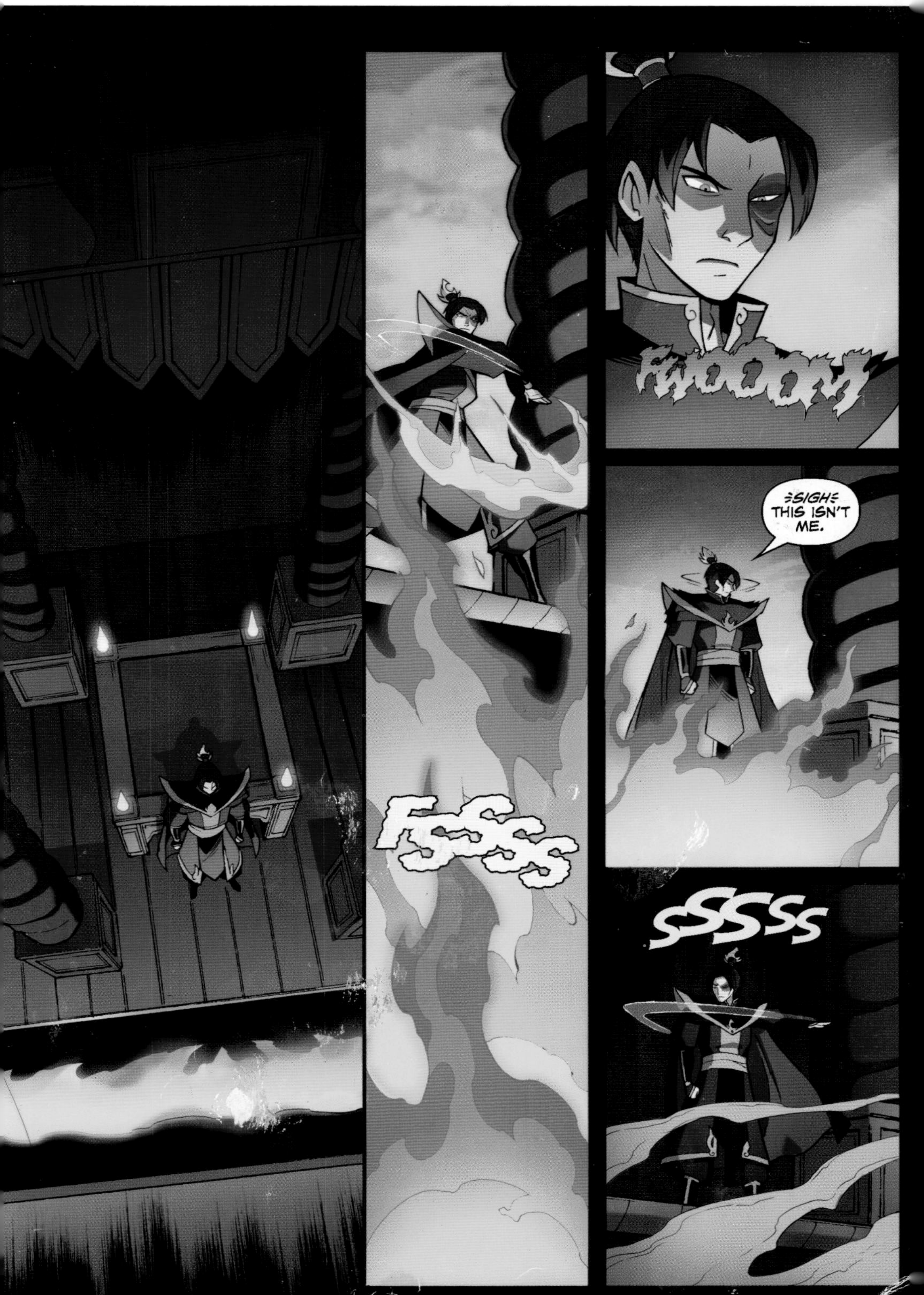
FSSSS
FWOOOM
SIGH
THIS ISN'T ME.
SSSSS

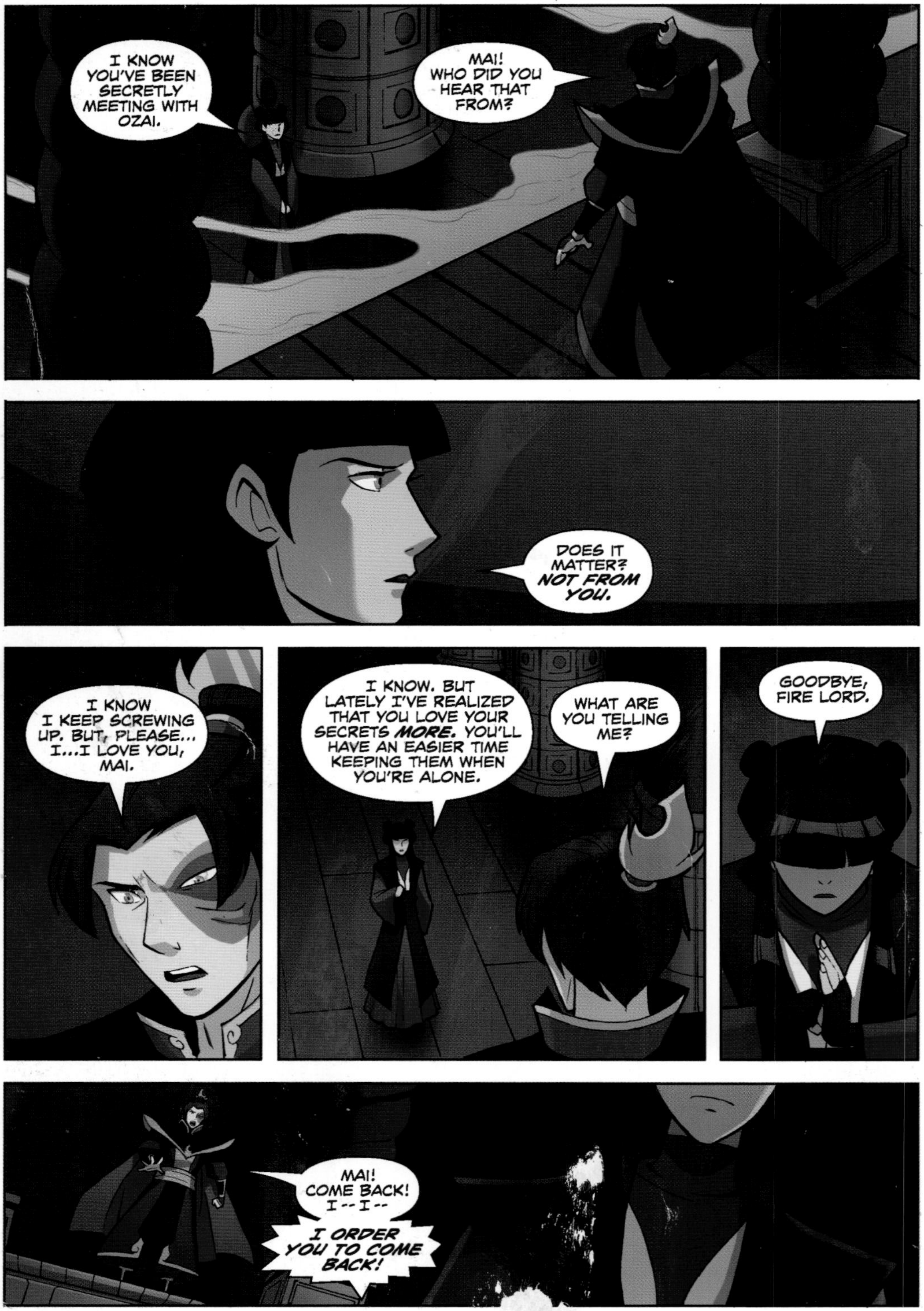
I KNOW YOU'VE BEEN SECRETLY MEETING WITH OZAI.
MAI! WHO DID YOU HEAR THAT FROM?
DOES IT MATTER? **NOT FROM YOU.**
I KNOW I KEEP SCREWING UP. BUT, PLEASE... I...I LOVE YOU, MAI.
I KNOW. BUT LATELY I'VE REALIZED THAT YOU LOVE YOUR SECRETS **MORE.** YOU'LL HAVE AN EASIER TIME KEEPING THEM WHEN YOU'RE ALONE.
WHAT ARE YOU TELLING ME?
GOODBYE, FIRE LORD.
MAI! COME BACK! I -- I --
I ORDER YOU TO COME BACK!

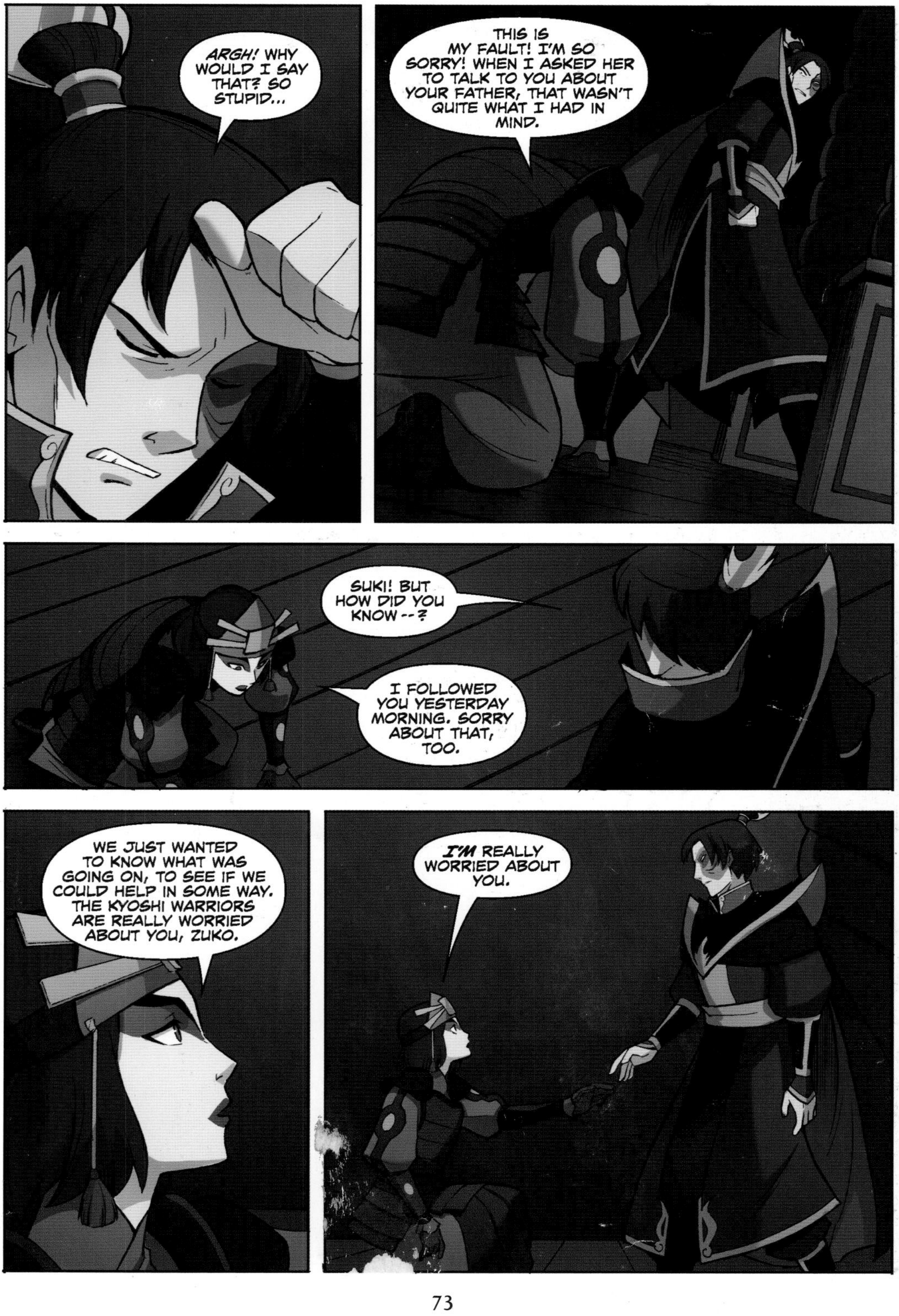
ARGH! WHY WOULD I SAY THAT? SO STUPID...
THIS IS MY FAULT! I'M SO SORRY! WHEN I ASKED HER TO TALK TO YOU ABOUT YOUR FATHER, THAT WASN'T QUITE WHAT I HAD IN MIND.
SUKI! BUT HOW DID YOU KNOW --?
I FOLLOWED YOU YESTERDAY MORNING. SORRY ABOUT THAT, TOO.
WE JUST WANTED TO KNOW WHAT WAS GOING ON, TO SEE IF WE COULD HELP IN SOME WAY. THE KYOSHI WARRIORS ARE REALLY WORRIED ABOUT YOU, ZUKO.
I'M REALLY WORRIED ABOUT YOU.

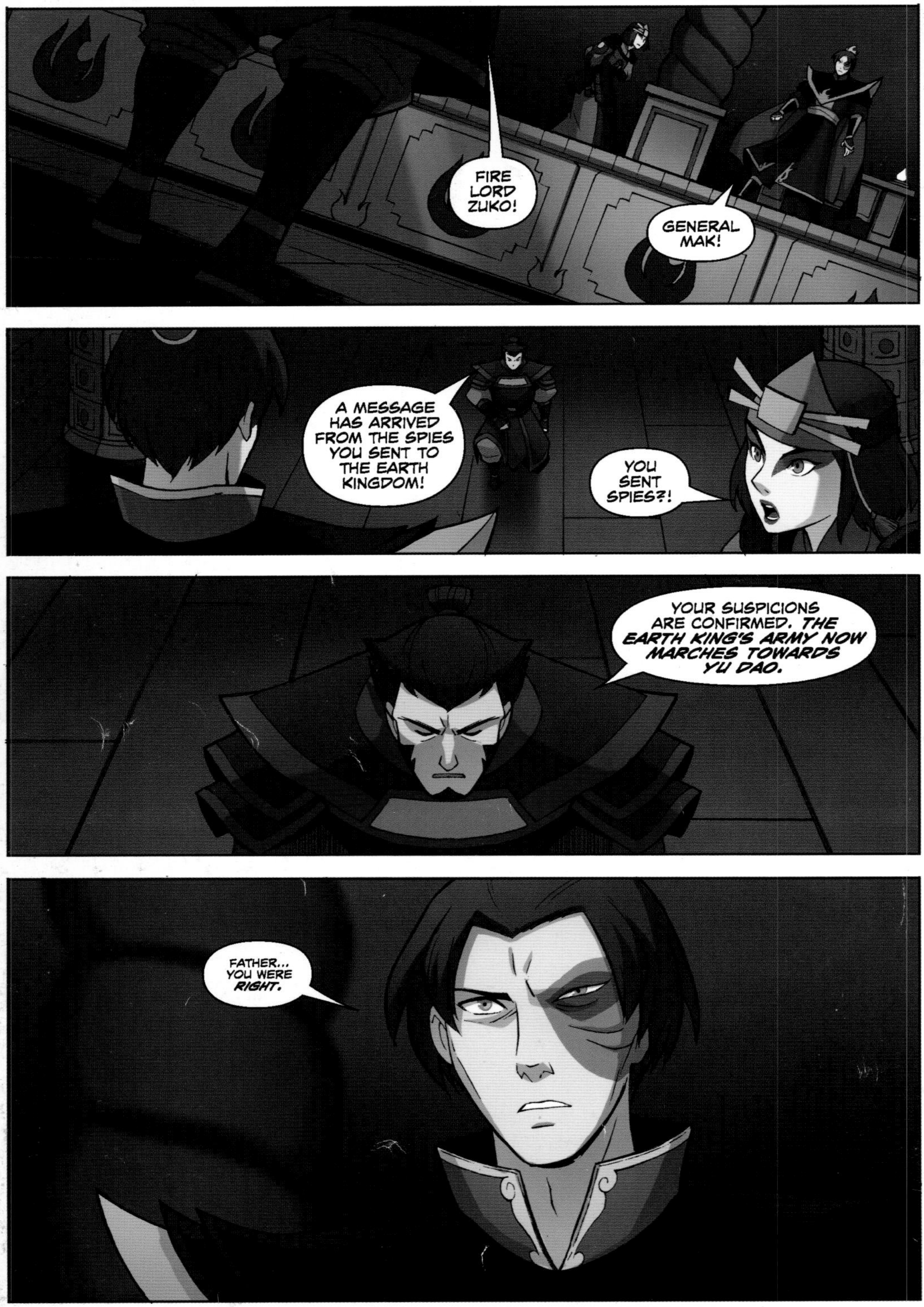

FIRE LORD ZUKO!
GENERAL MAK!
A MESSAGE HAS ARRIVED FROM THE SPIES YOU SENT TO THE EARTH KINGDOM!
YOU SENT SPIES?!
YOUR SUSPICIONS ARE CONFIRMED. *THE EARTH KING'S ARMY NOW MARCHES TOWARDS YU DAO.*
FATHER... YOU WERE *RIGHT.*

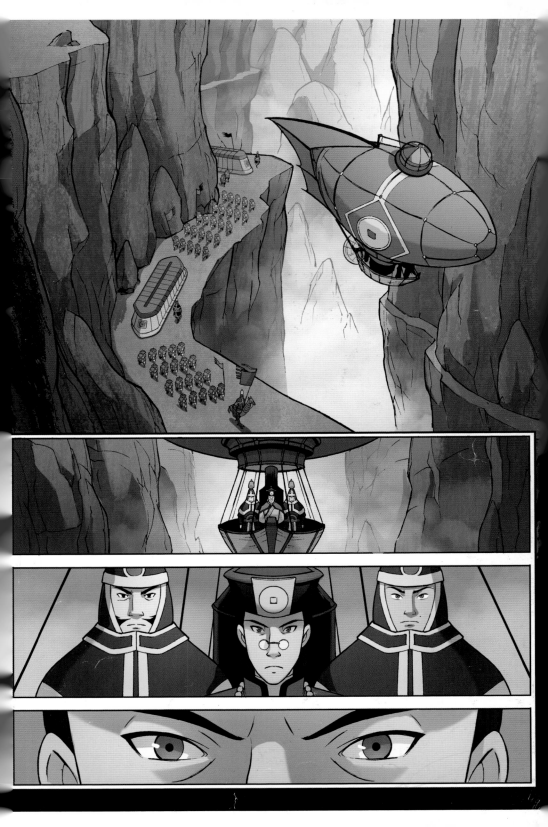

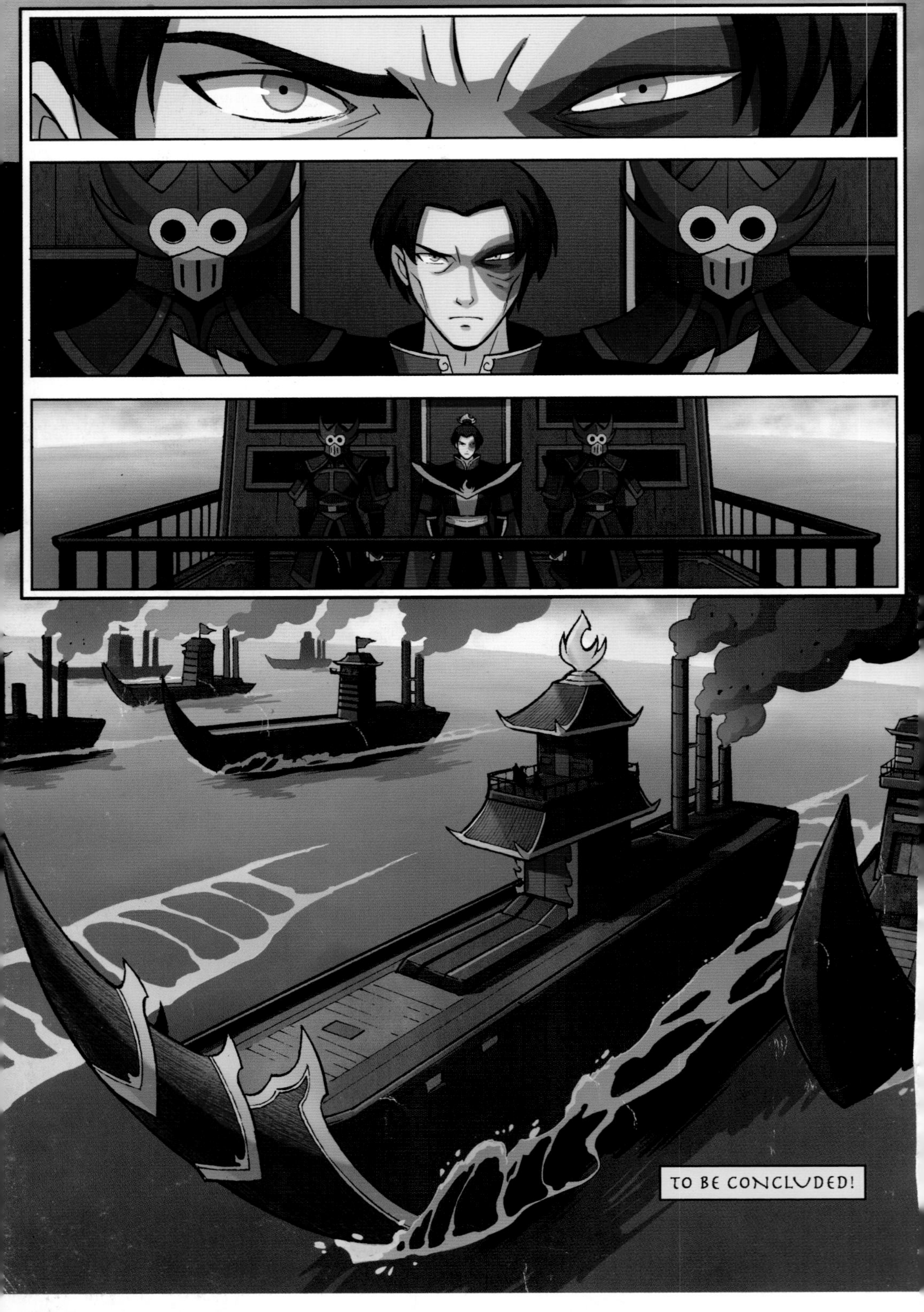
TO BE CONCLUDED!

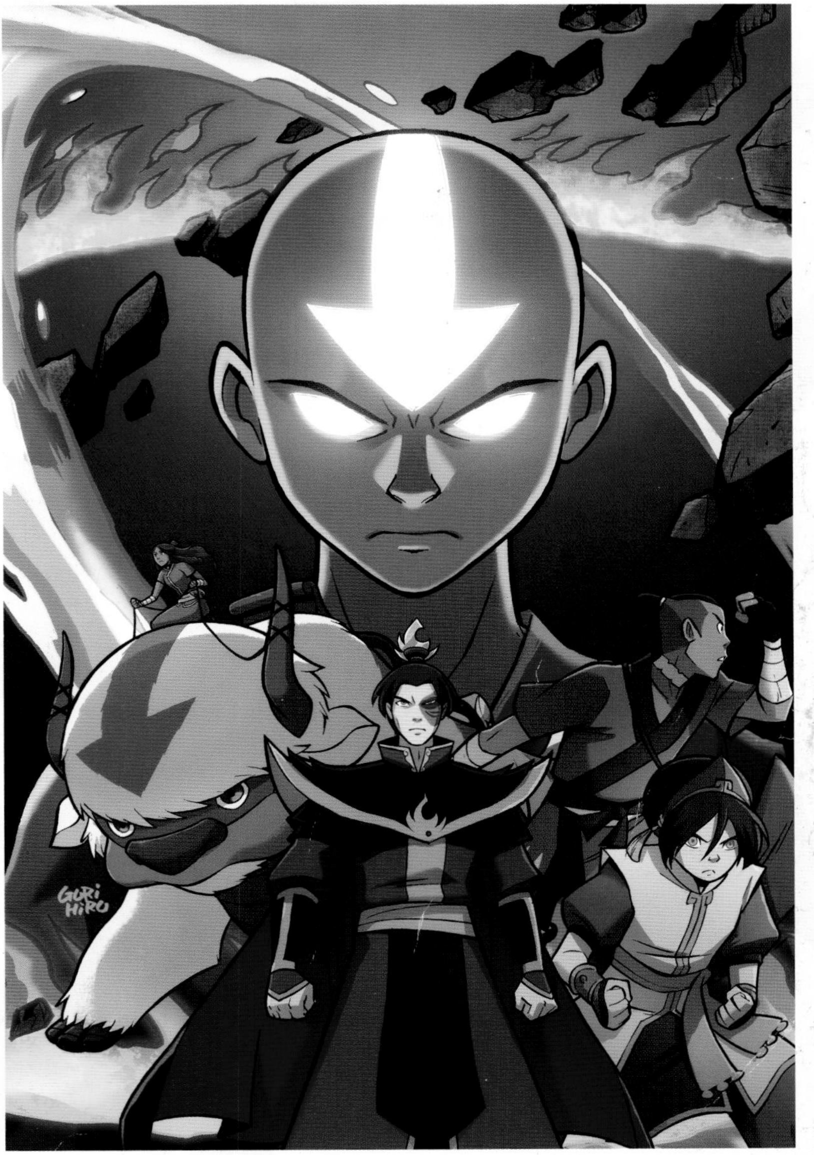
GORI
HIRO

COMING IN SEPTEMBER

Can war be averted?! Find out in . . .

THE PROMISE · PART THREE

ALSO AVAILABLE FROM DARK HORSE BOOKS

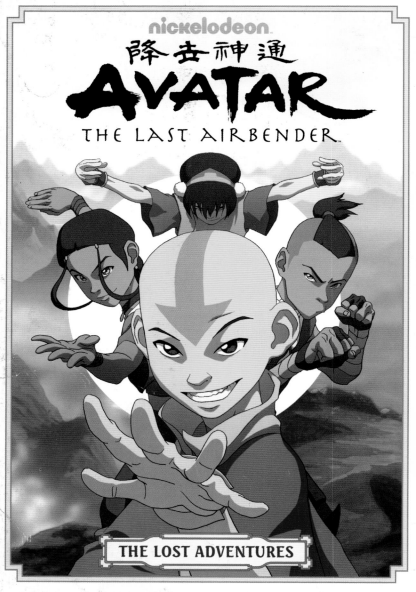

Twenty-eight stories set during the original three seasons, including over seventy pages of never-before-seen comics!

AVAILABLE AT YOUR LOCAL COMICS SHOP OR BOOKSTORE

To find a comics shop in your area, call 1-888-266-4226
For more information or to order direct, visit DarkHorse.com or call 1-800-862-0052

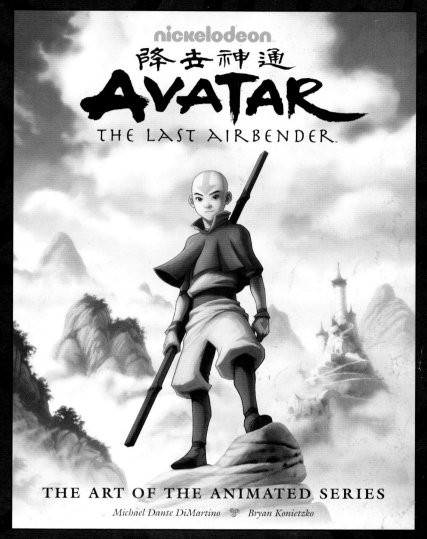